Nurturing Peace

*Theological Reflections
on Overcoming Violence*

Nurturing Peace

Theological Reflections on Overcoming Violence

Edited by Deenabandhu Manchala

WCC Publications, Geneva

Cover design: Marie Arnaud Snakkers
Cover photo: Peter Williams

ISBN 2-8254-1478-6

No. 112 in the Risk Book Series

Printed in Switzerland

Table of Contents

Acknowledgements

This book synthesizes the reflections and experiences of some one hundred theologians, social scientists, social activists and church leaders from all parts of the world who participated in a process of theological reflection on overcoming violence over a period of three years. A number of institutions and organisations have also offered their expertise and logistical support to the four consultations in Cret-Berard, Chiang Mai, Kigali and Oslo. Thanks to all of them.

A small group of theologians were called by Faith and Order to facilitate this process and articulate these reflections into this cohesive form. Therefore a special word of thanks and deep appreciation goes to the members of the Core Group:

Dr. Sathianathan Clarke, India; Rev. Araceli Ezzatti, Uruguay; Dr. Drea Fröchtling, Germany; Dr. Duncan Forrester, Scotland; Rev. Michael Markert, Germany; Dr. Janet Parker, USA; and Dr. Ann Riggs, USA.

Dr. Jione Havea, Tonga; Dr Sergey Hovorun, Russia, and Rev. Toma Hamidu Ragnjiya, Nigeria, who joined the July 2005 meeting of the Core Group in Geneva to produce this text.

Alexander Freeman for his efficient organisation of the consultations and for his careful and detailed work in finalising the text for publication.

Documents from this process of theological reflection on overcoming violence can be downloaded at:

http://wcc-coe.org/wcc/what/faith/nurturingpeace.html

All biblical quotations are from the New Revised Standard Version.

Introduction

The twentieth century was an age of great violence, and there are ominous signs that the twenty-first century may be even more violent and insecure. Time and again, as Christians attempted to discern the 'signs of the times', promises of hope were crushed by genocides, massacres, terrorist attacks, wars, global pandemics such as HIV/AIDS, hunger killing multitudes of children, and outbursts of lawless violence directed at innocent people.

The end of the Cold War and the collapse of communist regimes seemed at first to be unqualified good news, but it was quickly shattered by outbreaks of internecine violence in the Balkans, such as the massacre of some 8,000 Muslim men and boys at Srebrenica in 1995. In Palestine and Israel vengeance and retribution spiral constantly out of control, with rage and despair turning perfectly normal youths into suicide bombers, while sophisticated armaments supplied by western powers are used to devastate refugee camps and kill innocent men, women and children along with political opponents. In Indonesia, India, Nigeria and in many other places around the world, religion plays a major role in fuelling and perpetrating violence.

Soon after the terrorist attacks on New York and Washington on 11 September 2001 came the war in Afghanistan, and the daily horrors of the occupation of Iraq together with the ensuing civil war killing multitudes and destroying the basic infrastructure necessary for a decent life for ordinary citizens. The very values that the so-called 'war on terror' is supposed to defend are scorned in Guantanamo Bay, Abu Ghraib prison and many other places. Terrorist outrages, so fearfully unpredictable, mean that millions today walk in fear while their leaders seem incapable of prudent and just response. Countless civil wars and violent conflicts; a revived arms race and renewed drive for military security; and the proliferation and continuing threat of a variety of weapons despite international treaties continue to make the world an unsafe place for many. Rage, despair and immense cruelty seem to characterize the end of an era in which many people expected a new world order or – in the language of the Bible – the new Jerusalem.

Meanwhile, besides the visible and the striking, the phenomenon of violence itself has become increasingly complex, with challenges of a new kind. Some of these are the ever widening gap between the powerful and the powerless, the rich and the poor, further aggravated by the processes of economic globalization; increasing poverty and unemployment; millions being made refugees for various reasons; the glorification of violence by the media and entertainment industry; the rise of religious fundamentalism and growing intolerance; and the legitimization of all these implicit and explicit forms of violence against the innocent, the poor and the powerless, which indeed is a shameful feature of our world and generation.

There does not appear to be much good news around today. Instead, there is bad news in plenty. We all – Christians and people of other faiths – have immense difficulty in making sense of it all, in finding God in the imbroglio of today's events, in discerning the 'signs of the times', in daring to speak of and live out the gospel. But Christians believe in 'the gospel', that is, that there is in fact 'good news' today which they need to proclaim and offer, even – perhaps especially – in times of despair and fear.

And yet Jesus was born and raised, lived, preached, suffered, and died in an age with striking similarities to our own. The early church too proclaimed the gospel, the good news, with confidence and joy in a context of violence and despair. How is it possible to speak of God in this our world today after Auschwitz and the Gulag, after the Rwanda genocide, after the massacres in East Timor, and in the face of globalized terrorism and the bitter chaos that is Iraq today? How do we live out our faith in an increasingly unjust, violent and broken world? Can we recover the ability to discern and proclaim good news in a world of violence, despair and evil, where news seems invariably bad?

This is essentially the challenge that the *Decade to Overcome Violence: Churches Seeking Reconciliation and Peace 2001–2010* (DOV) poses to the churches. Declaring the Decade was indeed a brave and timely attempt by the World Council of Churches to meet that challenge. Some said that the whole idea was vastly over-ambitious and unrealistic. Certainly, if one judges by the amount of violence in the world, it would seem that the first half of the decade has been a failure. On the other hand, there is much to suggest that the Decade has enabled and encouraged the churches to become aware of the complexity of the global phenomenon of the culture of violence and to wrestle more strenuously with the realities of violence and conflict that surround them. It has also helped them to ask penetrating questions about the role of the Christian faith and the church in such situations and to look seriously at failures on the part of Christians and Christian communities in order to engage in a Christian way with the violence on their own thresholds, and even between and among them. The World Council of Churches, as part of its attempts to encourage and assist the churches, has been drawing attention to a variety of issues – international politics, economic justice, racism, violence against women and children, forgiveness and reconciliation in post-conflict situations, uprooted people, solidarity with peoples' movements, eco-justice, interfaith dialogue, peace education – and through all these the rationale for the ecumenical movement's relentless search for unity. Overcoming violence is thus a multi-dimensional task as well as a collaborative undertaking. To that extent, the DOV is an open space for the churches and all people of goodwill to come together to work for a better world – a world of peace based on justice, a vision that gives meaning and purpose to the Christian affirmation of faith in the God of life. Faithfulness to this God of life implies seeking peace in the midst of violence because it implies affirming life. The only alternative to seeking peace and the overcoming of violence is despair. Christians must hope with confidence, against all odds, for the coming of God's reign of peace in its fullness. It is this hope that calls them to be creative, to cross boundaries, in order to seek new coalitions for life and for a world that God wills and thus fulfil the prayer of the Lord, 'that they may all be one ... so that the world may believe that you have sent me' (John 17:21).

The Decade, therefore, is primarily an exploration in faith for a vocation of peace. However, churches have always stood divided and continue to do so on several issues that threaten peace and justice. Serious theological and historical hesitations inhibit the churches from taking a firm stand for peace. In fact it is often said that the churches have committed themselves to the Decade not because they have a solution, but rather because they realize that they have been a part of the problem and that they have to face it. During the Decade, the churches are called to reflect on their positions, attitudes and approaches, both positive and negative, to violence and peace, and to discover new theological bases for the pursuit of peace, justice and reconciliation, drawing from the wellsprings of scripture, tradition and experience of creative, critical engagement in the world.

In its relentless efforts towards fostering Christian unity, Faith and Order has been working not only on issues that keep the churches apart, but also on those that bring them together for greater expressions of visible unity. It recognizes that the issues of violence and peace are deeply theological and are relevant as well as necessary for the credibility of their witness to the gospel of peace and life in this violent world. Therefore, a small group of theologians from different parts of the world was called to develop and facilitate the theological work of the Commission on Faith and Order on peace. In 2003 this core group issued an invitational document: *Nurturing Peace, Overcoming Violence: In the way of Christ for the sake of the world*. Churches and ecumenical organizations in many parts of the world made extensive use of this document, which unpacked a number of theological challenges for the churches. The core group was responsible for accompanying a series of reflections on three specific themes: 'Interrogating and redefining power', 'Affirming human dignity, rights of peoples and the integrity of creation' and 'Realizing mutuality and interdependence in a world of diverse identities'. These reflections spanned over three years and involved over 100 theologians, biblical scholars, social and political scientists, human rights and peace activists and younger theologians from different parts of the world with their distinct contextual and experiential questions and perspectives. They were developed through consultations held in different contexts in the world in an attempt to learn from the complexity of the phenomenon of violence, from the successes and failures of the churches and Christians, and from the experiences of peacemaking and conflict resolution something of what God is doing in the world in these ominous and violent days. As such, these reflections were attempts to do theology in context and face to face with the experiences of violence.

The violence of the powerful, with the US military occupation of Iraq as a clear example, together with the rapid polarization effected by the processes of economic globalization, is an urgent thematic concern shared by the WCC and the DOV, which brought together a group of theologians and social scientists in Cret-Berard in Puidoux, Switzerland, in December 2003 to reflect on the theme 'Interrogating and redefining power'. This consultation highlighted four important challenges: to reclaim the 'power of interpretation' from the monopolizing powers; to 'democratize power'; to explore ways by which 'religion and power entail just peacemaking'; and the need to reassert life-affirming and liberative 'biblical and theological models of power'.

To reflect on the same theme and to react to the report of the Cret-Berard consultation, a group of younger theologians from Africa, Asia, the Caribbean, Latin America and the Pacific met in Chiang Mai, Thailand, in February 2004 and highlighted the need for a 'public theology for the twenty-first century', for 'the disempowered to assert their subjecthood', of 'being in solidarity with the social movements' and for 'discerning the nature of political witness of Christians in multicultural contexts'. They also affirmed the need to articulate a new ecumenical vision from the South.

When a group of theologians and human rights activists met in Kigali, Rwanda, in December 2004 around the theme 'Affirming human dignity, rights of peoples and the integrity of creation', they came face to face with the stigma of the Rwandan genocide, and were thus compelled to ask unsettling questions about the proper and actual roles of Christians and Christian communities in that unspeakable horror of massive abuse and destruction of life. While dealing with the detrimental notions of the Other, the consultation strongly reaffirmed the sanctity of 'every human being as the image and likeness of God'; highlighted the need to 'reweave the web of life' and to 'remember the victims of violence'; and called upon the churches to discover 'the meaning of being church' in a world that is led by values, notions and assumptions that promote fear, hatred and human division.

The conviction that the aggressive assertion of identities is a major cause of violence in many parts of the world today brought together another group of theologians and peace activists from nine specific contexts in Oslo, Norway, in April 2005 to reflect on the theme 'Realizing mutuality and interdependence in a world of diverse identities'. Their stories of overcoming violence in contexts where identities – social, religious, linguistic and ethnic – were used as instruments in the struggles for power and wealth on the one hand, and for justice and dignity on the other, influenced their theological reflections. They wrestled with the 'dilemmas of power' and the challenge of seeking 'unity amid increasing diversity', considered the theological relevance of affirming 'human vulnerability and the church's option for a kenotic existence' and emphasized the need 'to heal the trauma of violence' as an important way of overcoming the vicious cycle of violence.

This book presents and discusses some of the insights and challenges emerging from these processes as an offering to the churches and Christians everywhere. The members of the core group participated directly in some of these events, and exchanged and discussed reports and papers while accompanying the process. In July 2005, they met together in Geneva and identified three theological challenges for the churches and the ecumenical movement to consider as they participate in the Decade to Overcome Violence. The following chapters unpack some of the implications of these challenges.

I. Affirming Human Dignity and Integrity of Creation

I was a man, a woman, a child, a foetus. You know I was killed.[1]

I was killed by the militia because I am a Tutsi.

I was killed by the army because I was Hutu and a member of an opposition party.

I was killed by my neighbours because I would not go with them to kill others.

I was killed because I sought to protect my neighbour's child.

I was killed by my priest because it was the price he had to pay to keep others alive.

I was killed by my wife, my husband, my children, my parents because they had to kill me or be killed.

They killed many like me, women, children, men who happened to be here. I know why, but I don't know why.

I was buried here by my family.

I was buried here in this mass grave and no one knows whether I am dead.

I died here in my grave after they forced me to dig it and put me and others inside it and shot us.

I have never been buried. I am in my house. I am in the woods. I was thrown in a river.

I have been left here as a testament to what happened, for you and for the world to see.

The inhumanity we have known is human.

It is in our human differences that we have found reasons to dehumanize one another.

That is what I want to tell you.

We have died; we have killed because we are like you.

I am like you.
Now, I am dead.

Rwanda, where over 800,000 people were massacred in a period of four months in 1994 in one of the most shameful acts of ethnic hatred in recent history, a nation that is learning to respect the value and worth of every human being, was the site of the theological reflection on the theme 'Affirming human dignity, rights of peoples and the integrity of creation'. As one of the most distressing and challenging contexts, Rwanda points again and again towards the need for penitence and lamentation, and for healing and hope. It is a paradigmatic example of the violent convulsions gripping our world today and a fruitful locus for theological reflection upon peace.

Violence as violation

Ten years after these events, the Kigali consultation began on the basis of the following faith convictions:

- That all human beings – male and female – are created in the image of God.
- That human life is intricately interrelated with the rest of God's creation, and that human relationship with God is experienced and lived out in mutually interdependent relationships.
- That human beings are called to uphold the integrity of God's creation.
- That life is a gift of God and hence should not be abused.[2]

The contrast between these theological convictions and immersion in the context of post-genocide Rwanda could not have been starker. This painful paradox posits that churches immersed in a violent world begin from within a broken web, where creation's integrity is impaired and human dignity is constantly under threat. Therefore, the starting point for theological reflection is the reality of the violation of God's manifold creation.

Defining violence has its limitations. The term 'definition' itself entails the Latin term *finis*, meaning 'borderline', 'demarcation' or 'end'. The very character of violence lies in ignoring these borderlines, whether with regard to an individual, a family or a communal body. E. Milosić, a woman survivor of the genocide in Bosnia-Herzegovina, describes such violence as follows:[3]

> There is no way that you can define violence, because in a definition, there is a borderline and there is an end. But when it comes to violence, there is no borderline, and there is no end, because it is the very nature of violence that it respects no borders. You may think that your body is the outer borderline of who you are, but a soldier will come and invade that very territory of yours with his penis. And you may think that your soul is a sacred space, but then your husband will come and break into that very space by shouting at you and by calling you names. And you may think that your community respects your borders, your body and soul and all that, but then you find that it is your own people invading your home, taking all they want to take. That is why I say: there is no way to define violence.

If there is no way to define violence, is there a way to describe it? Descriptions require words, and violence often leaves a person speechless. Perhaps violence is in itself a *via negativa*, not in the classical epistemological understanding, but rather in concrete, existential terms: violence as an act(ion) that negates and refuses to see the humanity of the other person, and violence as an act(ion) that negates life in its fullness and its comprehensive potential for all. As such, the face of violence can be personal, structural, cultural or religious. On account of this complexity, violence is a reality that individuals, families, communities and nations all over the world experience in a variety of forms on a daily basis.

Violence, whether physical, structural, or psychological, and however it expresses itself, is a denial and abuse of life. Robert McAfee Brown's explanation of violence seems appropriate here:

> Whatever 'violates' another, in the sense of infringing upon or disregarding or abusing or denying that other, whether physical harm is done or not, can be understood as an act of violence ... While such a denial or violation can involve the physical destruction of personhood in ways that are obvious, personhood can also be violated or denied in subtle ways that are not obvious at all, except to the victim. There can be violation of personhood quite apart from the doing of physical harm.[4]

Racism, sexism, casteism, acts of invasion and occupation, unjust trade policies, etc., need to be seen as expressions of violation of the other. The fact that some are systematically made and kept vulnerable for abuse and exploitation makes the task of overcoming violence an important ethical and spiritual concern. Thus, the Kigali report stated:

> Violence ... is not only physical harm but also and essentially the violation of the personhood, of the rights and space of the other. So much so, the denial of the dignity of the other is both a motivation as well as the first casualty of any form of violence. Most victims of any form of violence are the innocent, the powerless, and the dependent, who in most cases are those whose human dignity is denied by religious, social, economic and political structures. Having been motivated by such attitudes, some pursue their rights to opportunities and security even to the extent of violating the rights and basic needs of others. That same logic is at the heart of the processes of increasing commodification of the human person and the earth's resources, the ethic of exploitation for economic growth, and the development ideologies that trample over the rights of the poor and destroy the earth, our common home.[5]

Recent ecumenical theological reflection has expanded the understanding of violence to include not only violation of human beings, but also violation of other life forms and of the earth itself. Most importantly, the interconnections between violence against human beings and violence against the earth have been recognized as inseparable dimensions of the abuse of power and the denial of the conditions for life. Human beings, created in the image of God, were not placed in a vacuum, but were situated within a wildly diverse and fertile creation which is blessed by God and endowed with its own intrinsic value ('And God saw all that he had made, and it was very good'; Genesis 1:31). The absolute dependence of human beings upon the earth as the source of life witnesses to the truth that 'the integrity of the creation is the framework within which we understand human dignity … the violation of the one involves the violation of the other.'[6]

This lesson was painfully demonstrated in Rwanda, as it is in all war-torn lands. The aggressors targeted not only the people themselves, but also burned fields and destroyed farm animals in a genocidal attempt to cut off people's source of sustenance. The integrity of the nation's water supplies was destroyed as hundreds of thousands of corpses were dumped into rivers and lakes, which ran red with the blood of the slain. Rebuilding efforts have caused mass deforestation in Rwanda and the loss of wildlife habitat. Indeed, 'war always leads to the devastation of people and the earth together, in a solidarity of suffering'.[7]

Terrorism and counter-terrorism activities, as two forms of violence plaguing our world today, also involve the violation of human rights and dignity, as well as the integrity of creation. A recent discussion document on terrorism, human rights and counter-terrorism developed by the WCC's Commission of the Churches on International Affairs asserts that both terrorism and certain counter-terrorism activities constitute an assault upon human dignity and human rights. While stating that terrorism can never be justified on religious or moral grounds, the document notes that the 'war on terrorism has in some instances corroded the very values that the terrorists target: human rights and the rule of law'.[8] The same document also observes that a UN report on terrorism issued in October 2001 states that efforts to fight terrorism must respect all existing human rights obligations under international law.[9] In addition to severe violations of human rights and dignity, terrorism and some counter-terrorism measures also destroy the integrity of creation. For example, the sophisticated ancient systems of water-harvesting developed over millennia in Afghanistan have been almost totally destroyed due to Afghanistan's tragic position at the centre of the current war on terror.[10]

Another devastating dimension of violent conflicts involves the distinct vulnerability of women. David Scheffer, former US Ambassador-at-Large for War Crimes, discussed the horrific practice of rape as a weapon of war and genocide in an address at Fordham University in 1999:

> In the past ... rape and acts of sexual violence against women went unrecognized and unchallenged. In many conflicts, some soldiers, perpetrators, and world leaders viewed rape as a fringe benefit of war, an unspoken perk. While some observers have dismissed incidents of rape, with the reason that men, or as so often seen, boys, simply get out of hand or out of control after a rough day on the battlefield, recent history has shown that organized, systematic patterns of rape are a component of deliberate ethnic cleansing. The world community, on occasion, ignored the truth that these acts are not simply acts of recklessness, but acts of torture.[11]

Rape, a perennial scourge of warfare and aggression, has finally been recognized by the international community to be a war crime which is often employed intentionally as a method to humiliate and destroy a population. The widely publicized use of rape in the Balkan and Rwandan genocides forced the world to grapple with systematic sexual violence against women as a tool of genocide. As Scheffer notes, rape and sexual violence were codified as a recognizable and independent war crime for the first time in the statutes of the International Criminal Tribunals for the Former Yugoslavia (ICTY) and for Rwanda (ICTR). These historic statutes now provide a basis in international law to view rape as a war crime. Many women in the Balkans and Rwanda live (and die) today with HIV/AIDS as a result of having been raped during these genocides. At the Kigali meeting Kasonga wa Kasonga's meditation on the biblical story of the rape of Tamar (2 Samuel 13:1–20) drew attention to the widespread rape of women in the ongoing conflict in his country, the Democratic Republic of Congo. Tragically, it has recently come to light that UN Peacekeepers have also engaged in rape and other abuses of women supposedly under their protection, such as trading food for sex. Kasonga said that if we want to affirm human dignity, 'we have to prioritize and affirm the dignity of women first'.[12] At the Oslo Consultation too, Bishop Kumara Illangasinghe told the following story: During the recent tsunami that devastated two-thirds of the coastal belt of Sri Lanka, there were many sad stories of abuse. A young girl was getting washed away and drowned by the tidal waves. A middle-aged man was able to save her life. However, very sadly, the girl shared a shocking story. She said, 'He saved my life, but having brought me out of danger, he raped me.'[13]

Human dignity in danger

Racism and ethnocentrism also lead to extreme violations of human dignity. The WCC document *Human*

Rights: A Global Ecumenical Agenda declares unequivocally: 'racism is a sin against God and against fellow human beings. It is contrary to the justice and love of God revealed in Jesus Christ. It destroys the human dignity of both the racist and the victim.'[14] The experience in Rwanda is a window into the underlying logic of dehumanization that often lies at the root of racism, ethnocentrism and genocide. The promoters of genocide in Rwanda published the infamous Hutu Ten Commandments, which denied the humanity of Tutsis and called upon loyal Hutus to show no mercy to Tutsis. Tutsis were called *inyenzi*, or cockroaches, and were also equated with snakes and with all forms of evil. A graphic illustration of this dehumanization was provided by Tom Ndahiro of the Rwandan Human Rights Commission, who told a story from his own personal experience of witnessing a Hutu man using human bones as firewood to cook his meal. In an ultimate expression of the objectification and dehumanization of another human being, the man said, 'Yes, they died, but why should they be wasted?'[15]

These reflections on various assaults on human dignity point to the fact that human beings constantly struggle with the temptation of 'othering', in which the dignity of certain human beings is denied because they are different in some way from the groups in power. The Kigali Consultation puts it succinctly:

> This trait has been the origin of many violent structures, cultures and values, such as racial bigotry, ethnic hatred, slavery, gender discrimination and many other forms of hatred and exclusion. This has also given way to the emergence of certain oppressive symbols and assertions of power, such as religious, ethnic, racial and linguistic identities, that are used by the vested interests to consolidate and multiply their hegemony over opportunities, privileges and power. Consequently, solidarity degenerates into selfish obligation to care for one's own group and into denial of responsibility towards

others. In situations of scarcity and intense polarization of interests, there arises the desire of the dominant group to monopolize the space and resources, and to 'cleanse' or 'purify' their society of the unwanted. Therefore, the shameful legacies of ethnic cleansing and genocide.[16]

Moreover, in this globalized world, there seems a prominent trend towards the increasing commodification of the human person and earth resources.

In theological language, violence is both a sin in itself and also the rotten fruit of the condition of sinfulness in which humanity languishes. However, it is the affirmation of the *imago Dei* that gives a reason for the evangelical hope to trust in the Prince of Peace as a divine partner in human efforts to achieve a just and lasting peace in the world. The ecumenical affirmation of human dignity, which forms the basis for a Christian understanding of human rights, has two primary theological roots. First of all, the first creation narrative in Genesis1:26–27 establishes that human beings were created in the image and likeness of God. This highly anthropological understanding of human life emphasizes the imperishable value of every human being before God. As a theological conviction it carries with it an inescapable political dimension. If every human being bears the image of God, no culture or belief is justifiable which holds any person as a means to an end, as disposable, or as having an inferior status due to an accident of birth, a disability, or even due to sin. In this regard, the Faith and Order Standing Commission in Crete asserted: 'The church will rightly defend the cause or dignity of one person against the antagonism or prejudice of a whole society, recognizing that the least or most isolated individual is infinitely precious in the sight of God.'[17] Furthermore, the Commission made the challenging claim that 'Christian faith forbids us ever to suppose that even the most obscene enemies of human well-being are not themselves made in the image of God. They remain human persons, neither to be exonerated from personal responsibility nor to be denied justice and humanity.'[18] In sum, 'the image of God, while it can never be fulfilled in an individual who chooses to be closed off from God or from the other, can never be effaced in any person.'[19]

This conviction has serious, practical implications for the treatment of perpetrators of genocide and other forms of violence. The dignity of human beings can be deeply wounded and the image of God distorted through sin and violence, but never completely destroyed. This theological conviction provides a solid grounding for strong human rights conventions, which ensure humane treatment of prisoners, including prisoners of war and war criminals. Christians who live in countries leading the current 'war on terrorism' have a particular duty to resist the use of torture by their governments, the increasing violations of fundamental human rights, and other governmental practices which violate international law under the guise of counter-terrorism or national security measures. It is heartening to note that as part of their response to the DOV, some concerned members of the Roman Catholic, Protestant and Historic Peace Churches in the US issued the following statement:

> We speak, moreover, in a time when the flagrant abuse of power has become evident in the sordid and cruel violations of human rights in US military prisons in Guantanamo Bay and Iraq. As US Christians, we are profoundly shamed by these violations of persons that have been perpetrated in the name of our country and in the pursuit of national security.[20]

Other people of conscience, including Christians in the US, are currently struggling to enact laws forbidding the use of torture under any circumstances and the practice of extraordinary rendition (which sends terror suspects to countries that use torture), and are seeking to investigate abuses of detainees and prisoners at Guantanamo Bay and in Afghanistan and Iraq. For Christians, these efforts may be aided by the understanding that human creation in the image of God is intrinsically relational. Since human beings are created in the image of the Triune God, Christians acknowledge that we truly image God only when we live in communion with Christ and with one another.21 This relational understanding of the human being entails constant effort to achieve reconciliation with our enemies. The essential human capacity for goodness and change needs to be affirmed even as acts and motivations of violence are condemned.

The second fundamental theological root of human dignity is present in the Christian confession of Jesus Christ as the incarnate Word of God: 'And the Word became flesh and lived among us, and we have seen his glory, the glory as of a father's only son, full of grace and truth' (John 1:14). In the person of Jesus of Nazareth, Christians confess that God assumed human form, uniting human nature with the divine life in a holy mystery. Thus, 'in faith, Christians look to a human face and in that face they see the image and glory of the invisible God.'[22] This points in the direction of the way each human being is treated. Not only did Jesus' nature as fully human and fully divine dignify humanity, but his ministry also enacted a profound solidarity with the marginalized and disempowered. Thus, 'As Jesus was found to be in company with people pushed aside in their own society, so our understanding of *all* humanity must be informed by our engagement with those whom society marginalizes.'[23] This implies the affirmation of the dignity and rights of every human being and a delegitimization of structures and cultures which exclude.

Finally, human creation in the image of God is intrinsically related to the God-given integrity of all creation. As the Faith and Order Standing Commission in Crete acknowledged: 'God created us to be in loving relationship not only with one another, but also with the entire creation … We are called to a relationship of loving care with the wider creation, acknowledging and taking responsibility for our place within the dynamic, interconnected and interdependent whole of creation.'[24] In Kigali, participants affirmed that 'creation is a living community of beings who sustain one another and are blessed by God'. Ivone Gebara describes relatedness as the primary reality:

> It is constitutive of all beings. It is more elementary than awareness of differences or than autonomy, individuality or freedom. It is the foundational reality of all that is or can exist. It is the underlying fabric that is continually brought forth within the vital process in which we are immersed. Its interwoven fibres do not exist separately, but only in perfect reciprocity with one another – in space, in time, in origin and into the future.[25]

In Rwanda, this concept of human beings living in dignity and in a healthy and harmonious relationship with the entire creation is expressed by the term *Amahoro*, the Rwandan equivalent to the biblical concept of Shalom. This harmonious concept of *Amahoro*, as well as the biblical witness to God's Shalom, is beautifully encapsulated in the Women's Creed, a statement written by a group of women from around the world in preparation for the UN World Conference on Women in Beijing:

> Bread. A clean sky. Active peace.
> A woman's voice singing somewhere,
> melody drifting like smoke from the cook fires.
> The army disbanded, the harvest abundant.

> The wound healed, the child wanted, the prisoner
>   freed,
> the body's integrity honoured, the lover returned …
> The labour equal, fair and valued.
> Delight in the challenge for consensus to solve
>   problems.
> No hand raised in any gesture but greeting.
> Secure interiors – of heart, home, land –
> so firm as to make secure borders irrelevant at last.
> And everywhere, laughter, care, dancing,
>   contentment.
> A humble, earthly paradise in the *now*.[26]

These reflections on affirming human dignity, the rights of peoples and the integrity of creation as a Christian response to build a culture of peace, point to three specific responses.

(1) Protection

We all need protection at one time or another: against danger, against enemies, against threats and against risks. Parents protect their children. Governments protect their citizens from external attack, crime and violence. And we all protect those we love and those for whom we have responsibility. But this justifiable responsibility is often pursued with the goal of a risk-free existence. It is based on the assumption that vulnerability is a sign of weakness. Unfortunately, this assumption makes some people callous and insensitive to others in the exercise of their power. Vulnerability is an important aspect of the human condition, a truth reiterated by the Oslo Consultation on 'Realizing mutuality and interdependence in a world of diverse identities'.[27] The recognition of one's own vulnerability can make one more humane, sensitive and compassionate towards others and their fears and needs. Children must be allowed to take reasonable risks if they are to grow up into responsible adults. In affirming human vulnerability, one begins to show signs of ethical maturity, in that one submits to the reality that one's own will and well-being can only be fulfilled in the well-being of others. A sense of adventure, the willingness to take risks, an openness to the new and the unexpected, and the ability and willingness to become vulnerable to others are all central components of a life that is worth living. Therefore, seeking protection through the exercise of violent power is a denial of the human capacity for negotiation and collective pursuits.

According to the biblical faith, ultimately 'God is our refuge and strength, a very present help in trouble. Therefore we will not fear though the earth should change, though the mountains shake in the heart of the sea; though its waters roar and foam, though the mountains tremble with its tumult' (Psalm 46:1–3; see also Psalms 62, 91; Isaiah 4:6). The Bible constantly affirms that God protects people against threats, danger and assault. In the Old Testament we read of 'cities of refuge' in Israel. Offenders, aliens and those being pursued for whatever reason could take refuge from their pursuers in these cities. The cities offered 'asylum' – a pressing issue in today's violent world (Numbers 35; Joshua 20, 21; 1 Chronicles 6-57, 67). For centuries, the church also provided sanctuary for people fleeing from pursuers who considered them, rightly or not, as criminals, enemies or undesirable aliens. The sanctuary was a holy ground on which people could take refuge. However, God's protection does not imply license for those who exercise their power irresponsibly. Ezekiel 34 condemns the custodians of religious order, as does Jesus (Matthew 23) for their abuse of power and for abdicating their basic responsibility to protect. It was sacrilegious for the knights of King Henry to slay Thomas

Becket on the holy ground of Canterbury Cathedral, and both the king and the perpetrators had to do penance for a particularly heinous crime: murder on the holy ground of a sanctuary, a place of refuge.

Neither a sanctuary nor what goes on within it can resolve the conflicts and offences that cause refugees to flee. But it provides a space, a pause, a period of time when things can be thought through and possibilities explored. A sanctuary may provide a time for healing, a time for reconciliation and a time for reparation. It does not offer in itself forgiveness and reconciliation and the healing of memories, but it may offer a hiatus until the *kairos*, the right time for the resolution of conflicts, the settlement of divergent claims and the dealing with offences arrives. Calling the churches to become sanctuaries of courage, the WCC consultation on 'Theological reflections on overcoming violence' in Colombo, Sri Lanka, in 1999 stated:

> We believe that we are called by the gospel to build communities characterized by honest, just and transparent relationships with God, in all its messy complexities; we keep company with those who struggle to overcome injustice and violence. The incarnate God is encountered in these hard places, and in communities (within and beyond the boundaries of institutional religion) which seek to integrate all the spiritual and material dimensions of God's creation.[28]

Sanctuary had a recognized place in premodern Europe. It still survives in some societies, and also in other religious traditions elsewhere in the world. The debtor is safe when he or she has reached the wall of the abbey-sanctuary. The suspected criminal cannot be arraigned or punished while he or she remains within the church precincts. The woman pursued by a drunken gang is safe when she reaches the threshold of the church. In modern times, although there is no longer a recognized system of sanctuary, many brave and wonderful people gave sanctuary in their homes to Jews fleeing from the Nazis, to refugees pursued by hostile authorities, and to strangers with no place to lay their heads, thus fulfilling the gospel saying: 'I was a stranger and you welcomed me' (Matthew 25:35). It is, surely, a continuing responsibility for Christians and the church, as well as nations, to provide refuge in times of unrest, violence and ethnic hatred, to those who walk in fear. There are heroic examples in modern times of those who have provided refuge at great cost to themselves. But there have also been too many instances in which there has been a refusal to offer sanctuary to those in desperate need of refuge. For Christians, one of the most tragic dimensions of the genocide in Rwanda is the fact that some ministers, priests and nuns delivered those who had come to them for refuge into the hands of their killers. Other Christians, however, went to heroic lengths to offer sanctuary to those fleeing the genocide. The violence against women and children and its legitimization in the church in many parts of the world is another shameful contradiction of this image of the church as a sanctuary.

In recent ecumenical conversations there has been considerable discussion about humanitarian intervention, especially because of its reliance on the logic and practice of violence, albeit to protect endangered populations.[29] Humanitarian intervention is often referred to as military action, usually under the auspices of the UN or another international body, to protect an oppressed or threatened community in a particular nation against the forces of its own government. It is regarded as a kind of police action. The evaluation of this possibility is often considered to lie outside the traditional parameters of the discussion of just war theory, which is concerned with warfare between nations or collectivities with a clear line of command.

Nevertheless, some just war criteria may be considered relevant to a humanitarian intervention which seeks to protect persecuted groups. Such an intervention, for instance, would be a matter of last resort only if all other endeavours to resolve the issue at stake have proved to be ineffective. The relief of the oppressed minority should not be taken as an excuse for a general assault on the offending nation. Innocent civilians should never be targeted. As Konrad Raiser has stated, 'A military intervention causing disproportionate numbers of civilian casualties and vast damage to the civilian infrastructure in violation of the Geneva Convention cannot be considered "humanitarian."'[30] The World Council of Churches, therefore, has opted for the term 'responsibility to protect' instead of 'humanitarian intervention' as a means to resolve the tension between the principle of national sovereignty and the responsibility of both governments and the international community to protect human rights and fundamental freedoms.

Although there are grounds to suspect that under the banner of humanitarian intervention some far broader economic and political aims have been pursued in recent times, it is also true that there has been some convergence between the two main approaches to armed conflict in Christian thought: the just war and pacifism.[31] Humanitarian intervention is seen by its supporters as a police action: loving neighbours by protecting them against attack, even when love has to be expressed through force, using as little force or violence as will serve the good purposes of neighbourly love. Not all force or coercion, of course, is lethal, but it is hard to draw an absolutely clear moral line between lethal and non-lethal force once one has admitted that force may sometimes be a necessary way of protecting particularly vulnerable people. This is not to say, of course, that violence, even lethal violence, is in some circumstances good. Indeed, many Christians are now coming to believe that all violence is sinful, but in a broken, sinful world, violence for the protection of the weak may well be necessary as the lesser evil. In such a situation those who use violence in a strictly limited way for the protection of the weak can fall back on the grace and forgiveness of God.

Yet if violence is occasionally necessary for the protection of the weak and the vulnerable, it is always hard to control responsibly, as it easily escalates. Therefore, it must be viewed and exercised only as a last resort. And in extreme cases, such as the massacre of Bosnian Muslims in Srebrenica or the Rwandan genocide, the refusal to intervene in a military way is culpable. General Romeo Dallaire, the Force Commander of the tiny UN Peacekeeping Mission in Rwanda, was denied the necessary military resources to intervene, and an overseas reconnaissance group told him: 'We will recommend to our government not to intervene as the risks are high and all that is here are humans.'[32] He concludes: "Ultimately, led by the US, France and the UK, this world body (the UN) aided and abetted genocide in Rwanda. No amount of cash and aid will ever wash its hands clean of Rwandan blood.'[33] Dallaire is clearly uneasy about the way 'peace-keeping' and 'humanitarian intervention' worked in Rwanda and elsewhere. He rather sees the task as one of 'mediating conflicts'. What is really needed, he suggests, is a new emphasis on conflict resolution, backed up by appropriate resources. Christians and churches that wish to protect the vulnerable cannot remain 'neutral and aloof'.

The church is called to generate a movement 'from hostility to hospitality in the whole of society'.[34] The way to that goal is long and winding, full of ambiguities and dangers, but Christians and Christian churches must tread that road with determination and confidence, relying constantly on the grace and forgiveness of God.

One cannot speak of protection today without addressing the issues around the challenge of upholding the integrity of creation. When God in the creation narratives of Genesis 1:26 declares that human beings are to have dominion over God's creation, it does not mean that human beings are given license to exploit and destroy the earth ruthlessly. The term dominion is to be understood on the biblical model of the ruler who is primarily a shepherd for God's flock, one who tends God's people and God's creation with gentleness as well as courage. The image used in Genesis 2 is even more telling. Adam and then also Eve are put in the Garden 'to till it and keep it', which can also be translated 'to serve and conserve' (Genesis 2:15), and presumably also to enjoy it and protect it. This understanding of human dominion over creation, which may be better described as human partnership *with* creation, is in a way reinforced and enriched by Jesus' words to his disciples:

> You know that among the Gentiles those whom they recognize as their rulers lord it over them, and their great ones are tyrants over them. But it is not so among you; but whoever wishes to become great among you must be your servant, and whoever wishes to be first among you must be slave of all. For the Son of Man came not to be served, but to serve, and to give his life as a ransom for many. (Mark 10:42–45)

In other words, Christians are called to be responsible stewards of God's good creation, serving the creation as well as the Creator God and their neighbours. They are not to be ruthless exploiters of what God has made. The earth needs protection, and its fruits are for reverent use and sharing for generations to come, and not for arrogant exploitation, indulgence and waste.[35] Therefore, supporting such agreements as the Kyoto Protocol and all other initiatives that resist pollution, waste and exploitation becomes an important way of expressing Christian commitment for the integrity of creation.

This is one way of repairing the broken web of life. Furthermore, the churches need to help their members to discern morally appropriate lifestyles that honour the well-being of all people, whether they are known to them or not, and whom they are morally bound to protect. Perhaps a theological reflection on the ethic of enoughness may be attempted, as a challenge to the over-consumption of the rich and as a genuine way of proclaiming good news to the poor. The churches are morally and spiritually obliged to protect life and uphold the sanctity of the creation; in doing so they witness to God who grants life for all through justice and peace.

(2) Protest and resistance

Even though protection (and advocating protection) of the vulnerable is an important responsibility of the church, protesting against and resisting the causes and forces of violence is necessary to overcome the spirit, logic and practice of violence. The church is called to protest and resist violence even in situations when it is unable to offer protection or when a particular government is unable or unwilling to protect those who resist violence. Protest and resistance are responsible forms of Christian witness in situations where violence is used as an instrument to deny and abuse life. Witnessing is an essential Christian function and one of the church too: 'And this gospel of the kingdom shall be preached in all the world for a witness unto all nations' (Matthew 24:14). Witnessing embraces both word and deed. In many Christian traditions, witnessing is also connected with martyrdom (the Greek word *martyria* means witness). The martyrs were primarily witnesses to the Truth proclaimed by Christ. From its very early years, the church believed that their martyrdom resembled the martyrdom of Christ, who gave his life for the life of people and whose death and resurrection confirmed the truth of his words. So it is *Christian* to witness; in other words, to deliver a *martyria* in a world overwhelmed by the forces of violence and death. And this *martyria* has radical connotations.

Facing the reality of violence, which in particular violates the dignity and value of human life, Christians are required to witness their opposition to it. Violation of life is contrary to God's purposes for the world. In doing this, Christians follow the example of the martyrs of faith and of Christ himself. Christians may witness in different ways. They may rebuke what is contrary to the message of Christ by words. Words are a powerful tool.

> Testimonies in the Bible show how words empower the poor and the oppressed. Psalms 9 and 10 are examples of that. These are full of words and expressions that describe both the poor and their powerful enemies. But both are written from the perspective not of enemies, but of the oppressed … These as well as others in the Psalter have become a 'zone of social possibility outside the theology of the powerful'. The Psalms, human words, converted into God's word, have the capability of empowering those in need, who suffer and are excluded, giving them the voice they have lost as a consequence of a deep experience of grief, depression and exclusion.[36]

'The Israelites knew what it meant to be suffering and to be silenced at the same time'. Psalm 137 is the story of a people unable to sing because of the experience of captivity. 2 Samuel 13:20 describes how the abuser told Tamar not to tell anybody about her rape. The concubine in Judges 19 experiences a traumatic silence after being abused all night. In the New Testament, in contrast with

Pilate's silence expressed through the washing of his hands and refusing to accept responsibility for justice, in the silence of Jesus, the silence of the innocent one, we recognize the counter-cultural silence that evokes the very truth that Pilate tried to run away from. There are enormous possibilities for the churches today to protest by speaking against the forces of violence, outbreaks of violence, the abuse of power and (most importantly) the culture of silence that legitimizes the violence of the powerful. As part of this witness, churches need to expose the hideous intentions of the powerful and the perpetrators, as well as appeal to the common sense of the communities involved.

'Active love' is an expression that is often used to insist on the need to witness through deeds. In particular, as described above, protecting the victims of violence may also be seen as Christian resistance to outbreaks of violence. Protection is a risky task. The grievous history of genocides, wars and other violations of human life and dignity provides innumerable examples of Christians offering protection for those suffering persecution. Often, they did so by putting their own lives at risk. In Rwanda, one comes across many examples similar to that of Paul Rusesabagina, a hotel manager who saved over 1,200 Tutsi people during the genocide.

History is replete with instances of Christians having to protect their homelands and their neighbours from foreign invaders. While this could be viewed as a fundamental national/patriotic response, Christians also need actively to confront those systems and structures within and through their countries and communities that dispense injustice and suffering. Christians are called to risk obedience for the sake of justice and peace, for the sake of Christ. In this way the document of the Standing Commission on Faith and Order 'Participation in God's Mission of Reconciliation – An Invitation to the Churches' states:[37]

> In many situations the decisions taken by powerful foreign countries, and by international organizations such as the World Bank, the International Monetary Fund and the World Trade Organization, need to be opposed. Some critics of these bodies contend that, through their policies and rules, they impose on individual governments a set of macro-economic measures which (according to the Trade and Development Reports of the United Nations Conference on Trade and Development) have led to greater inequality among and within nations, tending to weaken the poorer countries and sectors of society even further. Churches need to offer an informed and responsible critique of economic policies which increase inequality within and between nations. This too is part of the churches' work for healing and a just reconciliation.

In spite of a majority choosing to remain indifferent and unperturbed, it is heartening to note that many Christians in different parts of the world do protest against various forms of structural violence, social and economic injustice and abuse of power. Some join the ranks of people's movements and non-governmental organizations that struggle against the hegemonic power wielded by multinational corporations, international financial institutions and governments who exploit people and the earth for the sake of narrowly defined interests and profit. Some organizations of Christian women and churches have also spearheaded efforts to protect women from domestic violence, to provide education for girls and to change laws which discriminate against women. Many ecumenical organizations and church bodies such as the World Council of Churches advocate for just peace and the integrity of creation in international fora such as the United Nations. In these and many other ways, Christians launch a protest rooted in the heart of the gospel into the halls of power, with the unwavering message that violence is not an acceptable means of resolving our problems or of structuring our societies.

(3) Reconciliation and restoration

The experiences of those who have personally suffered the impact of violence in extremely destructive ways – those mutilated populations trying to reconstruct their lives, families and societies and to overcome their pain, hatred and desire for revenge – prove that violence defaces the humanity of perpetrators, victims and survivors. It defaces individual, family and community relationships, and it defaces structures like the global economy when the majority of earth dwellers are left alone outside the gates, excluded from participation in the economic *oikos* of our globalizing human society. It defaces culture that communicates identity and his- and her-stories when it is applied as a hegemonic, controlling force or as a (often traditionally legitimized) means of securing male-centred leadership. It defaces religion when an exclusionary vertical relationship is utilized to destroy horizontal relationships with fellow human beings.

In Christianity, the divine as well as the human face is of particular relevance. The face can indicate the presence of relationships as well as a withdrawal from relationships. Cain, for example, was no longer able to face his brother Abel after contemplating violence as a potential means of securing an influential position. And the psalmist pleads to God not to turn away God's face from those who approach God in prayer. In the context of the Hebrew scriptures, hiding one's face meant the breakdown of communication, a rupture in a relationship, be it with God or with human beings. If we can no longer bear the presence of a person, something is obviously wrong in our relationship. The expression 'Get out of my face' testifies to that. Facing the other always implies a certain openness towards him or her. Emmanuel Levinas, a Jewish French philosopher, claims that every encounter starts with facing the other. Many mis-encounters happen, willed or unwilled, because we do not face each other. The moment we look into another person's face, we are responsible for him or her because we have encountered a fellow human being with his or her hopes, fears, dreams, past and vulnerability. Faces as much as bodies are great communicators. Faces communicate a zeal for life or depression; they communicate joy or sorrow, and amazement or fear. Faces bring a person's inner being to the outside. When we fully face each other, we become involved in each other's lives, encountering each other fully.

In contrast, violence defaces; it dismembers peoples and communities in multifaceted ways. Violence denies the subjectivity and personhood of people; it denies mutuality and interdependence in human relationships. Violence leaves its marks, affecting body and soul, dreams and visions, trust and faith, and relationship and self-perception. The sinful human experience of violence and its consequences has to be examined by Christian theology in the light of the biblical witness and the church's history of witness to the hope of the coming reign of God. We must be wary of popular Christian teachings that offer quick fixes to traumatized people by either offering comfort at the end of time or with a glorification of the cross, through calls for martyrdom or the emulation of the sufferings of Christ. Widespread as these approaches have been, they generally prove more harmful than helpful. They often hamper straightforward efforts to deal with the causes and sociopolitical conditions of trauma and frequently lead to what Jeremiah 6:15 denounces as 'treating the wounds of my people carelessly'.

The Oslo consultation acknowledged the need for an encompassing response to trauma from the churches:

> In response to trauma, the church and its ministry should get involved in looking anew at diakonia, word and worship, pastoral care, education, stewardship and homiletics. All of these categories of ministry could and should be developed. Diakonia could include mediation, advocacy, and education ... The challenge is to prepare the people of God for ministry in a world of violence, restoring trust and relationships.[38]

Such a restoration of life is a religious task. The term religion goes back to the Latin word *religio*, which means 'to reconnect', 'to bind back' and 'to link again'. Religious communities, including churches, often seek such a reconnection in repentance, forgiveness and reconciliation. The invitational document 'Nurturing peace, overcoming violence' places primary emphasis on repentance as the prerequisite for overcoming violence:

> Repentance is both an act in humility lamenting kyrie eleison, seeking forgiveness for the sins of commission and omission, and an act of renewed commitment, to be open to new possibilities. Therefore, repentance for complicity in violence and apathy in resistance is seen as the necessary first step in the direction of overcoming violence in the world.[39]

Out of repentance come forgiveness and reconciliation. In this respect, one needs to be humble in soliciting forgiveness from a victimized person. Just as much as it is important to preach forgiveness, it is also equally crucial to encourage and impress upon offenders the need to *seek* forgiveness. Paula Coelho, survivor of rebel attacks on a village in Northern Angola, cautions:

> Churches, they always talk about forgiveness, that you must forgive because God forgives you. But I am not God, and if a guy who messed up my whole life just gives me a lame

'Sorry', then the burden is on my part to forgive and give him back a good conscience when he has just given me a word. In a church, if you say, 'no, I don't forgive you' … people will put pressure on you. I am ready to forgive when this guy has restored at least those things that can be restored to me and I will forgive at a time when I know. Now we are talking on eye level again. It's only when I'm remembered, when I am fully a member and subject again that I can forgive, otherwise it's a give-away, cheap grace. [40]

Forgiveness helps the victim to move out of the continued impact of violence. But unilateral forgiveness or attempts towards reconciliation without speaking the truth or dealing with the past can only amount to an endorsement of further violation. Paula's words demonstrate the truth of the statement in the Oslo document:

Forgiveness is often an emotive and misunderstood word. Forgiveness is not about forgetting, [… it] involves publicly naming the pain and the past. The act of forgiveness is actually an act of judgement. Forgiveness also has a political dimension and community responsibility. It will often involve the redistribution of power and resources.[41]

Forgiveness and reconciliation are long-term processes, often ruptured, often fractured, and seldom straightforward. They require changes in points of departure and perspective, changes in viewing the other, changes in sociopolitical, cultural and religious relations as much as in relationships on the individual level. They require a changed perspective on notions such as victim, perpetrator and survivor, and a vision that acknowledges the humanity and personhood of the other.

There are many positive roles that the church as an active partner in God's mission can play to bring reconciliation and healing in situations of broken relationships. The church can serve as a safe, healing space where people can engage in lament and truth-telling and hear one another; it can also be a space for difficult encounters between perpetrators and victims, and for modelling authentic forgiveness based on healthy remembering and true reconciliation rather than on cheap grace. As a worldwide community, theologically understood as the body of Christ in the world, the church is a radical space of encounter and dialogue for people of all cultures and nations. The members of the church are taught that when one member suffers, all suffer. This is a powerful incentive to work towards the restoration of broken relationships. Finally, the church announces the promise that God's justice will one day triumph over the suffering, the hatred, the death and the destruction of God's creation. The church not only remembers the harm committed through acts of sin, but also remembers the salvation wrought through the work of Christ. Thus, Christian life is an *anamnestic* or memory-filled experience based on the salvific remembrance of the new life in Jesus Christ, as well as on the memories of the individual person's life. As an anamnestic life experience which mediates between the tension of our current experience and our hope in Christ, the Christian life proclaims the hope that 'violence will be finite one day, finished, gone – and there will be an insurrection against violence that leads to resurrection, people who stand and walk upright once more, people who don't lose sight of each other.'

The gospel message makes provision for such a vision. It offers a framework for reweaving and reconstituting relationships based upon the notion of the *imago Dei*. It encourages the displacement of a culture of violence by a culture of sightful care when facing each other. The rabbi in a Hasidic tale asserts: 'When you look into the face of a person, the face of any person, and you see a brother or a sister in him or her, then, my friend, you know that the day has come and the night is over. Light has overcome darkness.' May such a day dawn upon us.

Issues for further reflection

1. Our homes, congregations, communities as 'sanctuaries' for those suffering from violence.
2. 'Humanitarian intervention' in today's world.
3. Practical ways in which Christians may exercise their responsibility towards the integrity of creation.
4. Derogatory and reductionist views of human nature which lend legitimacy to social and political powers.

2. Abuse of Power and the Church's Responsibility

> *Those whom they recognize as their rulers lord it over them, and their great ones are tyrants over them. But it shall not be so among you; but whoever wishes to become great among you must be your servant and whoever wishes to be first among you must be slave of all. (Mark 10:42–44)*

Power, an essential factor in all dynamics of human interaction, is increasingly sought after and exercised today in ways that seem to pose serious challenges to the ethical integrity of our generation, with implications for the present and the future, the personal and communal, and the local and global. The DOV, launched in a spirit of repentance for complicity in violence and of determination to overcome the spirit, logic and practice of violence, has helped the churches recognize that the roots of violence lie in the way power is understood, exercised, feared, coveted and glorified by the perpetrators, victims and even spectators of violence. As part of the world, the churches have been all these and have also been guided by the dynamics of power, cherishing and living with these orientations as well as ambiguities within and outside their realm. In spite of the consciousness of the biblical models for a responsible use of power,[1] instances of abuse and misuse of power in the church both in the past as well as in the present are manifold.

While this is so, the ecumenical movement in the twentieth century took its shape in a context of dominating yet changing power constellations. Its search for the unity of the church and of humankind has both echoed and challenged the dynamics of political and societal transformation. Konrad Raiser outlines three major phases. The first was the period from the Oxford 1937 Conference on Church, Community and State to the first Assembly of the

World Council of Churches in Amsterdam in 1948, during which the ecumenical discussion focused on the understanding of the state and the concern for the legitimacy or the limitation of its power in view of the emergence of totalitarian rule. This resulted in the first Assembly proposing a clarified concept of power through the definition of the 'responsible society'. During the second phase, ethical discussion was marked by the effort to interpret rapid social change. This implied a gradual shift of attention from the power of state and government to the new forms of power related to technological development and their capacity to orient and implement decisions. It also acknowledged the emergence of 'people's power' as a new reality. The third phase is in the context of the discussions on a just, participatory and sustainable society which upheld that the struggle for justice requires a new understanding and praxis of the political order and the use of power. This implied an exploration of options which Christians and churches must take in their political witness and of the biblical and theological bases for these. This phase culminated in the World Convocation on Justice, Peace and the Integrity of Creation in Seoul in 1990, which issued ten affirmations, the first of which was that 'all exercise of power is accountable to God'.[2] It must also be added that the ecumenical movement, whether as a mediator or a prophetic voice and (it has to be said) sometimes exposed to attempts of misuse by others and not sufficiently self-critical,[3] acted as a bridge between the powers that waged the Cold War.[4]

Today, the ecumenical movement is confronted with the necessity of exploring the means of bringing about a just, participatory and sustainable society in a globalized world with a new dialectic of power centres. Economic, military and political powers have each taken new shapes, necessitating the need for fresh analysis and theological reflection. The violence resulting from present global power constellations can be seen in the injustice evident in the global market, the control of resources, knowledge and technology, and the military might of the states of the northern hemisphere. These in turn are challenged by acts of terrorism, the privatization of power, the proliferation of weapons and means of destruction and the weakening of effective state structures, even international ones such as the United Nations.

The churches and the ecumenical movement do not stand outside these developments and are not exempt from the danger of perpetuating them, sometimes through the unconscious mirroring and sustaining of the power structures in our world today.[5] Yet they are called to be signs and instruments of God's reign of peace and justice and of a concept and practice of power that fosters the life and communion of all creatures. It is therefore necessary for churches to interrogate power in order to nurture a culture of peace.

Recognizing the increasing complexity of the emerging global order, the meeting of younger theologians from the South in Chiang Mai, Thailand, in 2004 called for a methodological and ideological shift in the way churches analyze, understand and interpret social dynamics and the scriptures.[6] This applies to power itself, both in the way in which it is understood and used in the scriptures and consequently practised in the history and life of the church. In their critical analysis of the way in which inherited images of a 'powerful' God were conceived in politically and economically powerful western contexts and used as mascots for colonial expansion and continue to be used extensively by the forces of global empire, these theologians said that cherishing these notions of God in a world where the majority are victims of power is not only a theological aberration, but also a betrayal of their hopes for justice and liberation. They pointed towards the need to redefine power and to reconstruct the images of God in ways that affirm the finer and life-enhancing attributes of God and God's purposes for the created order. In this spirit, this reflection on power is presented in a way that opens possibilities for more liberative interpretations and consequently more responsible forms of power.

It is with this conviction that the story of Hagar is used throughout the following discussion to clarify the arguments as well as to provoke fresh reflection on the interpretation of the biblical stories, which also include resisting certain interpretations and filling in gaps in the narrative. The story of Hagar and Ishmael, narrated in two parts (Genesis 16:1–16; 21:1–21), vividly portrays some of the major dynamics of power, both at the level of human relations and in the crossing over between the human and divine spheres. The power of stories is affirmed in biblical literature and reinterpretation has been practised in biblical traditions (including Midrash's playful interpretations and the Church Fathers' allegorical interpretations). Voices of lamentation, especially in Psalms and Lamentations and Job, inspired the calls that are found in this chapter.

The many shapes and faces of power

Power has many faces and shapes. On a very elementary level, it is an important and necessary dynamic and force in all natural and human relationships. It is the energy, the potential to act, to effect and to shape. In fact there is no human being without power. Power in and of itself is morally neutral. What makes power prone to abuse is not its exercise *per se* but the motive and manner in which it is exercised.[7] According to the biblical witness, this elementary power belongs to the very being and dignity of human beings. To be human means to be endowed with the power to name, enjoy and care for the created order (Genesis 1, 2; Psalm 8). And even if this dignity and creative power of human beings stands in tension with actual existential threats and realities, it remains one of the major affirmations of faith of the church.

A significant feature of the exercise of power in societies, however, is that it is often encountered in structures that exist and operate on the basis of the objectification of power (e.g. authority, law, forces), its internalization (e.g. loyalty, duty, fear of sanction) and the accumulation of the means required to wield it (e.g. money, resources, technology). Such structures of power appear to exist by accumulating and processing the means to legitimize and perpetuate themselves. They make themselves appear to be, if not God-given, at least naturally intended, and thus withstand all attempts to trace their true origins to the elementary power inherent in human individuals. It is in this sense that power is seen as problematic and dangerous in itself, which leads to the question whether power is a morally neutral instrument or the mere force by which something can be done.

> Such *dynamics* of power may be seen in the stories of Hagar. Sarah, for example, as a barren woman (Genesis 16), was seen in patriarchal societies as a woman with no power. When she became a mother, her power became oppressive (Genesis 21). In the stories of Hagar, patriarchy is one of the structures of power that led to Hagar being given to Abraham in order to bear a child for him. For Abraham, his name would have no future, without a son. By not questioning what was done to her, Hagar seems to have internalized this structure of power. Abraham accumulates 'means of power' through the birth of one son (Ishmael), then a second one (Isaac). [8]

In view of the complexity of power, in terms of the ways in which it is both perceived and exercised, it is

42

therefore necessary to explore alternative and transformative models. Possibilities towards such an attempt are
identified in the following four sections.

(1) The ambivalent relation between power and vio-
lence

The role of power is pivotal to the understanding of any
form of violence.[9] Violence, after all, is an exercise of
power over the powerless or retaliation to such power. The
exercise of violence by the powerful and to some extent by
the powerless may in fact indicate a lack of power and an
awareness that power might be exercised in quite different
ways which may, in turn, reflect the shallowness of value
systems which allow and attempt to justify such callous
and violent acts. Paradoxically, this is as true of the powerful as of the powerless and is indeed a manifestation of
lack of power, a lack of legitimization and a lack of capacity to explore and exercise measures and possibilities that
do not violate or diminish life.

> When we unleash dubious forces in the pursuit of worldly
> power, we ourselves become its victims. In the pursuit of
> wealth, military strength and other images of power, we
> actually become dependent on these images and lose our
> capacity to imagine and pursue more healthy alternatives.
> And when our limited images of power fail us – when,
> despite our wealth, we confront a host of seemingly irre-
> solvable social problems and humanitarian crises and when,
> despite our military strength, we find ourselves in
> unwinnable wars – we are reminded that our images of
> power are often, in fact, illusions.[10]

Moreover, to be in communication and nurture critical
discourse with the powers of today may be more crucial
than ever before, since contemporary structures of power
are often experienced as violent in themselves. In view of
the growing concentration of power into fewer hands at all

levels – local, national and international – and also the phenomenon of struggles for horizontal power, the question of who controls these powers or who has access to them is ever more pressing. Ken Booth observes: 'The drivers of the global economy (the principles of capitalism) and of the states system (the principles of political realism) represent the common sense of their structures because they embody the interests of the powerful, by the powerful, and for the powerful.'[11] He suggests that the instrumentality of power must be interrogated. When power is understood instrumentally, it is desired, sought and amassed for what it can do. The paradoxical nature of power must be understood: it is both an opportunity and a threat for its holders and for others.

Power sustains itself by dominating, possessing, manipulating and controlling people's lives and systems. One of the causes of these is the fear or awe that power induces. The sheer scope of this power decimates resistance even in the face of blatant victimization. Those who thus feel powerless and remain passive tend to deny their own capacity to resist, and their own innate ability to be innovative, and so are unable to hold the powers accountable. The church needs not only to encourage people to live up to the dignity and power that it affirms, but also to be wary of false claims of powerlessness. Instead, as the younger theologians from the south said in Chiang Mai, the church must look for ways to use its power in accordance with the gospel for the empowerment and full participation of people enabling them to claim their rightful subjecthood.[12]

In this world context, the church has the moral responsibility to explore and propose models of power that open alternatives to the use of violence. Constructive and sustainable change in the world has most often been brought about through non-violent rather than violent means. Non-

44

violent struggle shows that power, even when concentrated and focused, does not have to engage in violence to achieve its goals. Mahatma Gandhi's concept of *satyagraha* brought an awareness that there are other sources of power than the objectified and internalized structures of power, and that the person who is in contact with the spiritual source in its cause for justice and freedom cannot be overpowered. The churches need to strengthen their witness to the life and proclamation of Jesus, whose awareness of the already present as well as the coming reign of God was a feature of his challenging, non-violent ethics (Matthew 5–7). But even with non-violence as the preferential option, some would argue that there might be situations where violence is unavoidable and where responsibility for the life of people requires the use of force. In such situations, restricting the use of force to non-lethal measures and refraining from killing might still allow the possibility for shaping a situation.[13]

(2) Between structure and community: The dilemma of the church

Power, as it is in the world and in all human relationships, is also a complex factor in the life of the churches. Although aware of the Biblical models of responsible use of power (e.g. Mark 10:45),[14] the church both as institution and as people is often found wanting in responsible and life-enhancing models of power. Unfortunately, there has also been a significant trend towards adapting some traditions and practices in the Bible where the misuse of power is endorsed.[15]

Edesio Sanchez illustrates this point by means of an analysis of the confrontations of different notions of power in the Book of Judges.[16] Although women occupied important leadership positions that benefited the people during the period of Othniel to Deborah, during the period of Jephthah to Samson women became victims of the mis-use of power and violence (Judges 11–16). The people of God are often seen taking sides with violence; indeed, violence escalates as the Judges story develops. Likewise, certain conceptions of God, biblical images, ecclesiastical institutions, theologies and liturgies have been drawn from hierarchical notions of ordering and thus have become the dominant expressions of the church. The result is that the church is often oblivious to the dangers of absolute power. The following story from Sri Lanka helps to illustrate the dilemma of power:

> There was a king named *Alawaka*. He was very interested in hunting, as kings often are. One day, when returning from hunting, he was very tired, and rested under a tree after his meal. He fell asleep, but suddenly woke up with a shock; the devil, which occupied the tree, had come out and was ready to kill and eat the king. Now the name of the devil was also *Alawaka*. Then the king said, 'Hold on, my friend *Alawaka*, if you kill me and eat me now, your meal for today will be ensured. But let us make an agreement; I am the king and I will send a person to your doorstep to be killed and eaten every day.' The devil thought this was a good idea. And they made an agreement. Instead of nurturing and feeding the people, the king sacrificed his people to be alive and retain his power. But at the same time the king became the devil.[17]

Talking about the relation between power and pastoral care, Duncan Forrester says that the primary agent of pastoral care is the church, the 'Community of Faith'.[18] The Holy Spirit empowers the church to resist the misuse of power that exercises itself over others. The church is required to share power with others and is called to speak and promote love and forgiveness in a world that is ridden with violence and conflict. In other words, the church needs to offer alternatives to violent and life-diminishing ways of exercising power.

The church can act in a credible manner only if it addresses and repents of its complicity in the violence of the political, economic, military and imperial powers. This repentance is required not only for the crusades, slave trade and colonial conquests of the past, but also for its present collusion with unjust economic, political and military powers.[19] The church is called to be a community of peace that gives people hope and life; it must be one that fosters unity, upholds truth and strives for justice and fairness in all structures of human relationships. There is a long biblical tradition of wariness and critique against self-sustaining structures of power, beginning with the critique of the kingship in Israel (1 Samuel 8).[20] Resonating with this tradition, the World Conference on Justice, Peace and Integrity of Creation (Seoul, 1990) affirmed 'that all exercise of power is accountable to God. Therefore, we affirm that all forms of human power and authority are subject to God and accountable to people. This means the right of people to full participation. In Christ, God decisively revealed the meaning of power as compassionate love that prevails over the forces of death.'[21] The members of the WCC Central Committee in their message on the occasion of the launch of the DOV in 2001 said: 'The real strength of the church remains in the seeming powerlessness of love and faith. We must seek every day to rediscover and experience this power. Overcoming violence calls and challenges us to live out our Christian commitment in the spirit of honesty, humility and self-sacrifice.'

The church as an inclusive relational, dynamic, interdependent community is meant to be a working model of God's dealing with the world and humankind, manifesting to the world God's intentions. Whatever polity it takes, it should be communal, personal and collegial. The church, as a human institution, has some of the most powerful and some of the most powerless. Therefore, it is called to exercise power as

God exercises power, through servanthood. The church in the hospitality of its worship must reflect this open fellowship in Jesus.[22]

To sum up, the church must also be a well of empowerment, similar to the well in Genesis 21:

We have a glimpse of how the power of servanthood works to sustain life and bring hope in Hagar's story, where her eyes were opened and she was able to see the well of water through the ministering call of the angel of God (Genesis 21:17–19).

(3) Theological resources for the just and responsible use of power

Recognizing God as the source of power

God as the source of power calls us to an understanding of God as the Creator, who not only loves and cares for the world but who, as both transcendent and immanent in the world, is the very power of life that energizes the whole complex web of life. But God's energy has a purpose. The Creator God is to be seen as the God firing the world with the passion for justice, 'the power that both works for justice and makes it'.[23] This is God's Shalom, the well-being that is God's very purpose for the world, and a well-being that has justice at its heart.

Duncan Forrester tells of an occasion where a theologian, discussing the Nicene-Constantinopolitan phrase 'I believe in one God, the Father, the Almighty', was talking eloquently about God's omnipotent power. Suddenly, he was interrupted by an Ethiopian Metropolitan who 'clasped his arms in front of his chest like a mother cradling a baby and swayed gently from side to side' as he said, '*Pantokrator*, as all the Greek Fathers affirm, means that God holds the whole world lovingly in his arms and protects it, as a mother does with her child. God has the power he needs to care for the world. God is not an arbitrary despot.'[24] Indeed, when the prophet Isaiah envisions a new world and society, it is a child who is hymned as the one born to establish the world with justice and righteousness (Isaiah 9:6–7). In another song of hope Isaiah looks again to a new paradise which is 'the Messianic kingdom seen through a child's eyes' (Isaiah 11:6–7).

Such understandings counter any human claims to wield power over others with little regard for their well-being. A loving *Pantokrator*, on the contrary, speaks to those who are placed in positions of responsibility, giving them a clear mandate to exercise their appointed roles with care and concern for others. These understandings also run counter to any claims to use power for the exploitation of world resources, whether human or natural. It is a salutary reminder that care for the environment is a human responsibility with a divine mandate.

> This is the God who came to Hagar and her son in the wilderness when she had moved away from her child in despair, fearing his death.

God as the source of power allows us to understand God as ever present with us and present in the whole created order. In biblical language this is radically imagined as the presence of God's Wisdom – in Greek, *Sophia*, in Hebrew, *Hokmah* – who comes offering her invitation to all who would choose to live a life of Shalom. This is a God whose Wisdom celebrates divine power by bringing God's laughter and delight to the world (Proverbs 8:30–31). But it is also a divine presence that acts powerfully in the lives of those struggling to survive. Mary Grey recalls how in a later refiguring of *Sophia*, 'women in the death camps of Auschwitz kept alive the *Shekhinah* (Hebrew) face of God, the maternal face of God, through the humble, caring practices of women'.[25]

So, too, the angel of God, in the wilderness, spoke to Hagar of God's presence.

This power of divine presence speaks a counter-voice to any human powers that would silence joy in God's world and deny life to those whose ways differ from their own ruthlessly imposed orthodoxies. But this God of Shalom is also the God whose energy turns wilderness into a place of transformation, a place where humans may live peacefully with each other.[26]

> This is the God who was with Ishmael (and Hagar) in the wilderness. Sarah and Abraham may have carried the promise for Israel, but God was also with those in the wilderness, now also a place of God's presence, of God's nurturing power.[27]

So, too, the Book of Job, with its stirring and provocative divine speeches spoken from the whirlwind, is a reminder that God who loves the created world also loves the places and creatures of the wilderness. Here is the call to humankind, through the character Job, to reorder its imagination to allow respect for a world which does not set humankind and human ways at its pinnacle.[28] This is a counter-voice to all powers which exploit the resources of the natural world for human gain, in total disregard of the health and ecological well-being, the Shalom, of the earth.

Recognizing Jesus as the presence of God's power

If God as creator embodies creative ability, as the Cret-Berard report declares, then 'Jesus is the revelation of the fullness of God's power. So the mystery of incarnation is to be seen as a continuation of God's expression of God's intentions of power.'[29] In Jesus, God gives us a model of virtuous human living. In Jesus, we encounter God as self-emptying, as a servant and more so as a suffering servant (2 Corinthians 12:9; Ephesians 1:3–14; Philippians

2:5–11; Colossians 1:15–20). Jesus, the friend and dinner companion of the marginalized and the rejected, radicalizes the world's view of the powerful and their associates. Jesus, working to bring the world's margins to its centre, is the very *Logos* of God, the Word that is of and from God, the Word that invited and gave creation 'permission to be'; this Jesus is the Word of God in action, the Word of God's intentions of power in action. In this the church is called to a life of service at local, national and ecumenical levels.[30]

The life of Jesus manifests the servant nature of power and this needs to influence the church's understanding of its being and purpose in the world. Jesus' affirmation of the despised and the excluded, and his radical message of the coming reign of God, point towards a different conceptualization of power. The power of Jesus was not one of domination ('power over'), but of companionship and servanthood. This is the power that affirms and sustains life, and God's Shalom. 'Jesus' greatest manifestation of service and power' was demonstrated in his death on the cross, which 'became the exclusive centre of the Gospel that Paul called "the power of God" (1 Corinthians 2:1–5).'[31]

So Jesus continues to appear to the Hagars of the world, announcing the good news of God's way for the world.

The gospels record Jesus himself being confronted with the choice of opting for power and authority in worldly terms, but refusing such an option (Matthew 4:1–11; cf. Mark 1:12–13; Luke 4:1–13). On the contrary, as the Cret-Berard report continues, Jesus portrays the power of God as *kenosis*, as self-emptying. To that extent, the power of God as the suffering one is seen on the cross, where power is made perfect in weakness. This then becomes the pivotal point in understanding divine power, a power recognized in vulnerability.[32]

This again goes radically against all human pretensions to exercise power in ways that seek to overcome weakness or vulnerability by setting up worldly barriers between the weak and the powerful.

Recognizing the Spirit as the outreaching of God's power

As the Oslo consultation on 'Realizing mutuality and interdependence in a world of diverse identities' declared, the mission of the Spirit is to transform the world and all its structures and systems. Referring to Luke 4:18, 19, Johnston McMaster, in his presentation on Northern Ireland, said: 'Pneumatology is about social justice and there is no *koinonia*, the creation of the spirit, without solidarity with the poor and the vulnerable.'[33]

And yet, as Mary Grey notes, there is a paradoxical element to the power of the Spirit, in that 'she works in silence, in the waiting time, in unseen creativity and hidden depths, awakening mutuality and empathy, touching sensitivity and longing for wholeness. On the other hand, … she is a disruptive Spirit … fuelling a compassion that crosses rigid boundaries between hostile groups of people.' She is '"the Wild Bird who heals", calling for the end of the domination of those who exploit the earth and people alike'.[34]

> Again there are echoes of the angel of God who appears to Hagar, promising a future to a fleeing victimized servant, and of the God who is there with Ishmael and Hagar in the wilderness as a God whose advocacy is for the crossing of all boundaries, symbolized in this narrative as those between Israel and Egypt.

Such an understanding of the work of the Spirit encourages a strong counter-voice to challenge those who would set up hostile barriers against people they would decry as 'other'. As the Oslo document advocates, this speaks to the need of the church to be viewed 'as a site of radical partnerships and as a potentially revolutionary site of social transformation'.[35]

Recognizing the Trinity as the power of God-in-community

Trinity as the power shared within the Godhead, in the moving, pulsating, self-encircling of the divine, permeating the world with God's purpose,[36] is a profound model of mutuality and interdependence as well as diversity.

> The unity of the Triune God is the perfect expression of unity in diversity. All men and women are created in God's image. Our differences, including our differences of gender and cultures, reflect God's plan and will. Diversity, therefore, is the self-expression of God. The image of God in human beings is a call to grow in the likeness of God. In the process of growth, interdependence among creatures is God's plan for the sustaining of life.[37]

This is an expression of God as a breaker of boundaries. Trinity understood as God-in-community also lays bare and counters all attempts by individuals or ruling elites to claim and exercise exclusive and oppressive power over others.

(4) Empowering to overcome violence

The Decade to Overcome Violence and the recent WCC documents addressing issues of violence and power,[38] in their overlaps and aggravations, oblige the ecumenical community to empower people and churches towards a responsible use of power that enables a just and equal distribution of means, resources, space and products.

The WCC is not alone in this calling. Similar voices to empower the weak and the vulnerable can be heard in many societies and cultures, from various people,[39] with different intentions.[40] Overwhelmed by structures and cultures that dominate and discriminate, the world today deprives many of the opportunities that life and the world offer to them. Access to opportunities is necessary for human fulfilment, as these provide possibilities for exerting power to resist and to seek safety. In fact, most victims of any forms of violence, including that of the violence of nature, are the poor, the weak and those who have been systematically disempowered by social, political and economic structures. Empowerment of the weak and the vulnerable, therefore, is an essential step towards the overcoming of violence. However, the call to empower also has paternalistic undertones and hence needs to be viewed and effected with care. The traditionally disempowered communities do need wider solidarity which can help them prevent themselves from falling victims to the vicissitudes of the times and social dynamics. Calling for empowerment rings loud in contemporary contexts, also: from the mass graves resulting from the devastation of the tidal wave of 2004 in Asia and the victims of hurricane Katrina in USA in 2005, to the killing fields of Iraq; from the sinking shores of low-lying islands, to the smoke-filled London Underground of 2005; from the ashes and scars of Rwanda, to the lashes in Guantanamo Bay, and beyond.

Consequently, we must define the targets of empowerment we encourage. This is necessary because, through the ages, structures and cultures have empowered some people to destroy peoples and identities, to terrorize and occupy their lands, to extend their own ideologies, to enforce social divisions and hierarchize societies, and so on. We do not endorse moves to empower that lead to the misuse and abuse of power. What we call for is the empowerment of people and churches towards affirming life, accountability and mutuality, interdependence and Shalom.

It is of course one thing to talk about empowerment and another to walk in its way; and one thing to empower and another to empower towards particular goals. In other words, we call for empowerment of people and churches to build fires, not for (self) destruction but for warmth, light, feasting, sharing and creating a space where Shalom is forthcoming. Empowerment must make people innovative and responsible. Empowerment is a double-faced concept, one of complexity and ambivalence at the same time.

With the consciousness of these limitations, the purposes of empowerment may be understood in the following ways.

Empower to survive

A popular Tongan saying, '*E 'ikai mākona ha taha 'i ho'o* (a hungry person cannot be satisfied or fed by your sermons/words), stresses the urgency of the call to empower people to survive, especially the disempowered and the excluded. This is a call to action beyond mere affirmation.

> From the story of Hagar and her young son, this is a call for the messengers of life to come and revive the lives of the dying Ishmaels of the world (cf. Genesis 21:15–20). This is also a call to the world's leaders, the 'gods of history', to look at the faces of grieving mothers, the faces of the world's Hagars, to put an end to the policies and actions which lead to, and perpetuate, violence against children.

In the face of the acceleration of violence and abuse of power, the first call is for empowering to survive. Empowering to survive is safeguarding life from abuse and destruction. Empowering to survive needs to be the primary vocation of the church, which confesses its faith in the God of life who came to earth to grant life, in all its abundance, to all people. In other words, the church should have the courage to leave aside its theological, institutional and cultural hesitations and justifications for inactions for the sake of the survival of the exhausted victims on the underside of history. The church should not let its own survival be more important than that of those who are denied life: the Hagars and Ishmaels of the world. The call to empower to survive testifies that ethics should always be foremost,[41] and embodies the call by many liberation critics for *praxis* before reflection.[42] The call to empower to survive is a call to embrace, to cuddle, nurse and protect life.

There is a subverting quality to the call to empower to survive. It is an instance of resistance, for in empowering to survive we frustrate the power of oppressors. In empowering to survive we declare that oppressors do not have power over the lives of people. Victims, like Job, shall rise from the ashes of history.[43] Victims, like Hagar, shall walk away from fear and despair. Accordingly, the call to empower to survive is a call to hope. When this call is embodied, given a body, it becomes a call to hope. In other words, the call to empower to survive and embody survival is apocalyptic in the biblical sense of the term. It is transformative both in the present and for the future.

Empower to name

An often-unexplored act of crime in contemporary times is what may be labelled 'identity theft'. This label comes from the world of credit and banking, where it refers to a thief using the identity (i.e. name, social security number and address, all easily retrieved from the Internet) of other persons, dead or alive, to run up a credit account or obtain a loan. What is stolen is the identity of the robbed person.

There are other forms of this dehumanizing theft. One is the denial and withholding of people's names and identities. There are many instances in the biblical narrative in which characters are nameless. The story of Jephthah's daughter (Judges 11) is one notable example. She is not named, even though she is a full character and plays a significant role in the plot of the story.[44] Since she is not named, she has been denied her identity as a distinct human person. A contemporary example of this is evident in the movie *Rabbit Proof Fence* (Miramax, 2002), which deals with the *stolen generation* in Australia. This too is identity theft.

There is yet another form of identity-theft: denying to certain people (mainly because of their gender, class, race, sexuality or age) the privilege of naming and thereby fulfilling an active role in determining their own reality and future. While the names of some of these characters are given, as in the case of Hagar (Genesis 16, 21), they are not granted the power of naming and deciding their reality and future.

> Hagar is named but Sarah, Abraham and the messenger of God determine what awaits her and her son in the future. Hagar, however, poses an interesting complexity because even though she is robbed of the chance to name her realities and her future she ends up naming God (Genesis 16:13).

It is because of such an ambivalence that we call for empowerment to name, encouraged by the fact that a character that is denied the privilege to name in one sphere is able to name in another. In this connection, 'the powerless' too have some form of power.[45] Accordingly, in order to counter the various forms of identity theft, churches need to 'empower people to name' by knowing them by their names, as real people, and respecting the names they give to reality.[46]

Empower to live in solidarity and interdependence

One of the consequences of the obsession with the self characteristic of the Enlightenment and presupposed in the two concerns discussed above, is the reassertion of the spirit of individualism in many spheres of life today. This happens at personal and public levels. Such public-level individualism is seen all too often in the parochialism which sets up barriers to keep differences at bay. On an international level it gives rise to ethnocentrism and justifies colonization. A man looks out for himself alone; the family becomes nuclear; city-dwellers are ignorant of what it means to live in the countryside; a church cares only for its own members and emphasizes the imaginary and unhelpful divide between the sacred and the secular; a nation provides only for its own interests; and so forth. These forms of individualism store and spread the seeds of violence and terrorism because they thrive on detrimental notions of the other.

Shalom, therefore, is possible when people are in solidarity with one another and affirm their mutuality and interdependence. This is the ecumenical vision of 'power with' (versus 'power over') that the younger theologians from the South advocate.[47] This vision calls for greater awareness of the relationality of life, the realization of justice and the redistribution of power in all structures of human relationships.[48] This means that the church needs to be more public and engaged with the world, ready to form partnerships with all those who yearn and work for justice for all.[49]

> 'Power in relation' ... taps the power each of us has to transcend the boundaries of our own lives, overcome our fears and take collective risks. When exercised with those committed to non-violent transformation, power is not seized by a few, but shared and exercised by many. By being inclusive, such power can lead to the common good. By being restorative, it enables old enemies to address painful histories, make amends, and create a peaceful common future for their children. By being transformative, it allows us to change our own thinking, inspired and supported by the insights and

strengths of one another, and to be liberated to think and act in new ways.[50]

In the story of Hagar, for instance, God does not work only at home, but also in the wilderness; the private and the public overrun; in other words, the secular is sacred.

The attempt towards empowering to live in solidarity and interdependence is not limited to marginalized people. It needs to go as far as requiring the privileged to face the disturbing presence of the marginalized and enable them to be in solidarity with the marginalized. This is necessary because if solidarity and interdependence were directed only at the victims and the disprivileged, then it might imply the continued individualization and fragmentation of human communities.

Empower to question and redefine power

Silencing dissent is an ongoing feature of all human relationships at every level. A form of censure that crosses cultures is contained in the phrase 'stop being a smart-ass' (Hausa, Nigeria: *Mai wayo*; Tongan: *Fie poto*). In some cases 'stop being a smart-ass' is actually used appropriately, but more often than not it is used to silence people and to deny them the chance to interrogate and redefine their realities, in the interests of leaders who cannot cope with their own vulnerabilities and feelings of insecurity. Silencing people is an act of denying personhood and human dignity. Churches need to identify and expose cultures and structures that justify and perpetuate such practices.[51]

This also points towards the need to redefine the structures of power in all contexts. It also requires that people are enabled to resist the ways in which they have been conditioned to read their sacred scriptures and accept their religious traditions. In this regard, we echo urgent calls recently given by many men and women from 'the South' to resist oppressive powers and symbols. There are two tones to this call: first, it is a call to redefine and reinterpret canons that legitimize oppressive structures of power;[52] second, it is a call to resist imperializing practices of oppressive powers.[53]

But responsible forms of power are necessary to sustain and protect peoples, as well as to enable development and effect change. In some churches, there is also a tradition of ministering to the powerful and to power structures with a view to counsel, encourage and allow repentance in difficult, complex and sometimes morally ambiguous situations. Such ministering may not avoid conflict and the suspicion of being supportive of existing power structures, yet it might well be a way of communicating the gospel in spheres that are important for the well-being of the world. In other words, speaking to the powerful and holding them accountable is as important and necessary as empowering the disempowered.

The call to empower people and churches to interrogate and redefine power is therefore liberative. It arises out of a state of subjectivity because the one who interrogates and redefines is one who *names* and is *named*. It is in this regard that empowering to interrogate and redefine presupposes having been empowered to name.

Empower to exercise power responsibly

Given the leanings of humanity towards what Martin Luther saw as a fallen state from which we cannot escape during this life, it is necessary to name and empower those forms and expressions of responsible use of power.

Every person has some form of power, but not every person uses that power responsibly. Irresponsible use of power has produced violence in families, communities, nations and the world. The Preamble to the Constitution of UNESCO states 'that since wars begin in the minds of men, it is in the minds of men that the defences of peace must be constructed'.[54] Since violence is produced in human minds, both intentionally and unintentionally, peace can also be nurtured and spread through human intentions and actions. It is our responsibility to one another to use our powers responsibly and it is the responsibility of the church to empower to exercise power responsibly.

Herein lies a critical response of the church. The church must repent of its participation and complicity in irresponsible uses of power – from the concentration camps of Europe, to the genocide church-sites in Africa and the atomic weapons testing holes dug in the Pacific. This call for repentance and responsibility comes loudest from the so-called 'mission fields' into which the church arrived under the protection of colonialism. Church and state arrived as a couple, hand in hand, cutting and digging to establish themselves at the expense of local and native folks and cultures. It is therefore necessary for the church to admit its moral responsibility for its past and present irresponsible uses of power.

Empowering *to exercise power responsibly*, therefore, must start at home. This means the church must start from within. This is the pastoring role of the church,[55] which must develop its caring presence throughout a world in which religious bodies share in the shame of fuelling violence.[56]

Issues for further reflection
1. A redefinition of power that can defuse the fascination with violent power.
2. Responsible and life-enhancing ways of exercising power at personal and collective levels.
3. Jesus' model of power of service as a means of social transformation.

3. Being Peacebearers, Becoming Peacemakers

> Rats and roaches live by competition under the law of supply and demand; it is a privilege of human being to live under the laws of justice and mercy
>
> Wendy Berry

The desire for invulnerability and self-sufficiency, together with arrogance stemming from the awareness of power, are in the background of most acts of violence. These aspirations make people aggressive in their own pursuits, even to the extent of violating the space, rights and dignity of others. This tendency to pursue one's own growth and fulfillment of desires by excluding and manipulating the other is present at all levels of human relationships. Wars, policies, structures and cultures are often the means used by the powerful to overcome vulnerability. In contrast to this arrogance and aggression to recreate the world to serve them, there is also the compulsive negative energy of insecurity. Thus, the fear and anxiety experienced by the powerful needs to be seen as part of this analysis of violence. This takes on added significance in our increasingly pluralistic world in which the aggressive pursuits of the preponderant spark violent struggles for identity and justice on the one hand and for power and resources on the other. Relationships of dominant vs. dependant, thus created, exploit identities of race, class, caste, gender, religion, language and ethnicity and brutalize human society, generating and perpetuating endless cycles of violence. The same narrow, selfish pursuit is also evident in the violent ways in which humanity continues to relate with the earth and its life-sustaining systems.

Through a convenient strategy that opts to be extremely parochial or exclusively spiritual or deliberately neutral, the dominant streams of world religions and their corresponding cultures have often failed to create and sustain values that uphold human interdependence and mutual responsibility in the current ethos of increasing fragmentation and polarization. Even traditional Christian faith expressions have not proved to be different. In spite of the strong accent on the love of the neighbour as decisive for a relationship with God, popular notions of salvation as ultimate in the human quest for fulfilment seem to be moulded by this spirit of individualism and the consequent social indifference that it legitimates.

Therefore, overcoming violence involves dealing with worldviews, attitudes, aspirations and conceptions of the other that influence human relationships. By being also integrally interrelated with all that is interconnected in the One who creates, liberates and sustains all of creation, it is rooted in God. Can an ethic of mutuality and interdependence respond adequately to the phenomenon of mutual fear and hatred that dominates our lives today? What are the implications of such an ethical responsibility for the churches' own existence?

Belonging to and longing for peace

Overcoming violence is both a goal and a process because peace is a condition of belonging and a state of longing. It is a condition of belonging to each other as children of God in relatedness with all of creation. It is a state of longing that joyfully joins in preparing for this eventual condition of relational blessedness – the grand reconciliation (Ephesians 1:10). Christian discipleship, therefore, is an invitation to be both peacebearers (bearing the marks of belonging to each other as children of God with all creation) and peacemakers (seeking the fruits of the condition of blessed relatedness in the spirit of active anticipation). Being intimately related to God as children is pivotal to the vocation of being peacebearers and peacemakers. Jesus extends this call to his disciples in the words, 'Blessed are the peacemakers; for they will be called children of God' (Matthew 5:9).

If upholding the sanctity and integrity of life is crucial for the affirmation of the Christian faith, can this global trend of fragmentation and violence on account of human greed, arrogance and fear be a reason for churches to consider the vocation of peace as a faith imperative, to be peacebearers and peacemakers in the world? Is it possible to see peacemaking as a *status confessionis*?[1] It seems necessary that the church embrace this vocation for the sake of the credibility of its existence and witness in today's violent world. But it is also important not to separate this call and commission of the church from what the God of Peace is already doing in the world. Nikos Nissiotis' reflection concerning the unbreakable bond between the church and the world expresses both caution and opportunity:

> We should not think that churches are going to create renewal processes in the world. Renewal in the world is a permanent event ... The church as a witnessing service to the world has to recognize this 'autonomous' event as happening also within the grace of God – of course, with the restrictions imposed by the historical predicament of human sinfulness. We should not posit an opposition of sacred and profane renewal, but an irreparable co-belongingness within the one creation which is in permanent process of renewal. The church as sacramental reality and vision is in the midst of this renewing process of all things, and must always be the primary reality of a world which is changing and renewing itself. It does this by sharing in this renewal through the people of its day.[2]

Violation and violence have spread at an alarming rate around the world as a threat to our peaceable *oikos*. The world is truly and hurtfully divided. While often interpreted along the faultlines of North and South, West and East, rich and poor, white and black, men and women, and privileged and deprived, the world is broken up into numerous fragments manipulated by several abusive social actors. Of course, on the whole, most forms of violence are more systematically, severely and pervasively felt by the poor and the deprived living in the global South, with a heavier burden resting on their women and children. This does not mean that horrendous violence is not perpetuated in the global South against its own peoples, nor does it imply that there are no victims of violence among the wealthy and privileged global North. It does mean, however, that violence is systemically more prone to affect those who have less social, economic, political and military resources, even though those who have power over such resources are still vulnerable to violent attack. Thus, while this divide is globally structured in terms of the North and South or West and East, it can also exist regionally and in fact at all levels between those who have unfair access to power and those who have marginal contact with such resources.

Violation and violence against all strivings to be part of a free and equitable relationship in God, with each other, and with all of creation is an assault on life as gifted to us. Peacebearing and peacemaking as a Christian calling thus minimally involves opposing and transforming forces of violence that undercut the ability of peoples to live in freedom and dignity and optimally involves strengthening all efforts that work for the furthering of life for all.

The biblical traditions inform the church's knowledge of peace in many different ways that describe the richness of the biblical vision of Shalom. Isaiah prophesies that when the Lord establishes his rule, 'nation shall not lift up sword against nation, neither shall they learn war any more' (Isaiah 2:4). In Isaiah's vision, the 'peaceable kingdom' is characterized by justice, righteousness, joy, enlightenment, knowledge of the Lord, the fruitfulness of the earth and satisfaction in human work (9:2–7; 11:1–9; 65:17–25). When this vision comes to fulfilment, human parents will not 'bear children for calamity' (65:23), for 'they shall not hurt or destroy' (65:25; cf. 11:9).

In his person, in his coming in the flesh, in his life, death and resurrection, Jesus Christ inaugurates this kingdom (cf. Mark 1:14–15). In him, Isaiah's vision has been fulfilled (cf. Luke 4:18–21). 'In him all the fullness of God was pleased to dwell, and through him God was pleased to reconcile to himself all things, whether on earth or in heaven, making peace by the blood of his cross' (Colossians 1:19–20).

The church claims that Jesus is this Prince of Peace that Isaiah had prophesied about (Isaiah 9:6). Jesus, in turn, sanctifies the vocation of peace-making through his own proclamation: 'Blessed are the peacemakers, for they will be called children of God' (Matthew 5:9). In teaching us to pray, Jesus teaches us to call for the presence of the 'peaceable kingdom' on earth. In praying for the coming of God's reign, we pray for peace.[3] The peaceable kingdom is already present and yet we await it, crying '*Maranatha*, Come!' to the Prince of Peace (Revelation 22:20). Therefore, we belong to and we long for peace. This is at the heart of our faith tradition, and at the centre of our story of faith.

For this reason Jesus called his followers the 'salt of the earth', 'the light of the world' and 'the city set upon a mountain top' (Matthew 5:13–16). They are called to transform and be transformed. Baptism is a sign of this kingdom.[4] In baptism by faith we participate in the benefits of Christ's own overcoming of violence on the cross and in his resurrection from this violent death.[5] 'The one, holy, catholic and apostolic church is sign and instrument of God's intention and plan for the whole world. Already participating in the love and life of God, the church is a prophetic sign which points beyond itself to the purpose of all creation, the fulfilment of the reign of God.'[6]

Viewed in the light of its centrality to God's intention for all things, to God's means in carrying out God's plan for the reconciliation of all things to Godself in Christ, and viewed in the light of its centrality to the faith, baptism, eucharist and ministry of the church, peace appears as a sign and instrument of God's Kingdom. In bearing peace and making peace, the church manifests its nature and carries out its mission as itself, being sign and instrument of God's love. In peacebearing and peacemaking, Christians enjoy a foretaste of the peace of God's holy mountain. 'How beautiful upon the mountains are the feet of the messenger who announces peace, who brings good news, who announces salvation, who says to Zion, "Your God reigns"' (Isaiah 52:7).

Again and again, communities of Christians fall short: 'the way of peace they have not known' (Romans 3:17). These failures to make peace, to live peace, to *be* peace, call for lamentations and repentance, which include our complicity in violence and our apathy of being guilty bystanders.[7] These failures contradict the unity, holiness, catholicity and apostolicity of the church: 'The oneness, holiness, catholicity and apostolicity of the church are God's gifts and are essential attributes of the church's nature and mission. However, there is a continual tension in the historical life of the church between that which is already given and that which is not yet fully realized.'[8] Hatred and violence rooted in disordered appropriations of ethnic and national identities stand, in memory and in present-day experience, between communities of Christian believers, contradicting the unity of the church manifest at Pentecost.[9] Meeting in the context of Faith and Order in the USA, representatives of widely different Christian traditions were able to say together: 'We are agreed, on the basis of the Apostolic Tradition, that Christians, following our Lord and Saviour Jesus Christ, are called to be peacemakers. We consider this a common confession of the faith once delivered to the apostles, basic to our Christian unity.'[10]

The vocation of being peacebearers and peacemakers today involves being sensitive and creative in various historical situations. And yet any exposition cannot ignore the general divide between the wealthy, privileged and powerful on the one hand and the poor, deprived and less powerful on the other. A theology of peace for our world today demands an honest and nuanced theological response to our increasingly complex world situation. Theological reflections that are open to demanding conceptual obligations in relationship to our complex contextual realities can be instructive as we carry out our mission of peace in the world as we know and see it today. Three brief theological mediations register the complexities surrounding us and what is involved in clarifying our role as peacebearers and peacemakers in the world.

Peace mediates between justice and forgiveness

Peace is not a state of escaping the real world of violence, strife, exploitation and injustice to seek solace in a virtual world that is entered into through imaginary leaps, even if propped up by 'feel good' gestures or by invoking the terms 'hope' or 'pilgrimage'. Rather, peace engages the real world to usher in the condition of belonging to each other as children of God in relatedness with all of creation. Peace as a web of relatedness (belonging) is thus intimately connected with peace as a process of complete, though differentiated, integration rooted in God (longing). It is recognizing and affirming the relationality of life. In such a realistic understanding of peace the notion of justice is unavoidable. It is in fact crucial. This universal yearning for justice is at the heart of the biblical vision of peace. 'To make peace, we must strive for justice. The vision of justice we set forth is holistic and social, rooted in the biblical vision of *shalom*.'[11]

Injustice is a common cause of violence. The powerful and wealthy resort to violence to contain the assertions of justice from the poor and the dispossessed. In some cases the victims – the poor and the dispossessed – also use violence to disturb the security of the privileged. Ironically, in our historical context, competing notions of justice feed rather than check violence. This can be seen at a global level, where there is an explosion of tragic, indiscriminate and horrific violence. On the one hand, terrorists are doing violence to people for the sake of certain notions of justice that they fabricate and hold onto according to their religious, national or ideological interests. On the other hand, globalizing agents of occupation and expansion, along with state-consolidating repressive forces, are violently and doggedly killing and penalizing peoples in the name of future freedoms.

In view of this increasing assertion of violent power, it is high time that the elements and consequences of justice become prerequisite to any valid discourse of peace. This alone can provide a comprehensive framework that stresses our mutual, interdependent and integral relatedness in God, to each other and with all of creation. Justice is an important face of peace and the praxis for justice must always accompany peacebearing and peacemaking. This involves 'an invitation to the churches to live a theology of peace as a sign of the coming reign of God – God's new order, and to keep, as a sign of solidarity, the experience and the visions of the victims of violence and injustice always in the foreground.'[12] Uncoupling justice from peace will unseat the poor and the disempowered from their blessed position in the Kingdom of God and subvert the life-giving objectives of the biblical vision of Shalom. And pursuing peace without justice will only result in false peace that will either soon be disrupted or turn destructive.

Forgiveness is another face of peace. Forgiveness is not about being misled into setting justice aside, but it saves justice from the destructive path of blind retribution. It allows for the possibility of realizing mutuality and interdependence in a world where competing justices generate violence rather than peace. The path of forgiveness in a journey of peace with justice allows for freeing both the destructive rage of the poor and the dispossessed and the immobilizing guilt of the wealthy and the powerful. Forgiveness cooperates with justice for the sake of peace through a process of rebuke and repentance.

> Forgiveness is not about forgetting, but it is about remembering in a way that does not close the possibility of rebuilding trust and relationship ... The act of forgiveness is actually an act of judgement. Forgiveness also has a political dimension and community responsibility. It will often involve the redistribution of power and resources. This underlines the close connection between forgiveness and justice.[13]

Peace mediates between security and vulnerability

Peace is possible when it is pursued towards the goal of mutually interdependent relationships. The Faith and Order study document *Church and World*, noting the family-like qualities of mutuality and interdependence (found in such passages as Galatians 6:2: 'Bear one another's burdens and so fulfil the law of Christ', and Philippians 2:4: 'Let each of you look not to your own interests, but to the interests of others'), suggests that one way to think of the peace of the kingdom is an application of these same characteristics to 'relationships within communities, within and between nations, and with the whole created order'.[14] Recognizing and affirming vulnerability, therefore, is a precursor for this process of reweaving this web of life, of humanization, and for the discovery of a new social order.

The Oslo consultation on 'Realizing mutuality and interdependence in a world of diverse identities' in April 2005 pressed this insight into situations where local churches are themselves challenged by violence in settings of ruthless individualism and lack of interdependence in the face of diverse identities. The theme proposes the ethical challenge of realizing mutuality and interdependence as a creative way by which churches can counter the reality of mutual fear and hatred dominating our lives today. The theoretical framing of the event was elaborated by Raag Rolfson in terms of mutuality and identity of human persons: 'If you recognize the call to goodness issuing from the nakedness of the face, subjecting you to responsibility, then you recognize that this is not just any call, not just any summons. It is what calls me back to myself, even prior to my freedom, claiming it at the same time that it is constituted.'[15] The participants brought with them their stories, observations and analyses relating to mutuality, interdependence and identity of communities.

For instance, Alina Patru, reflecting on the peaceful and mutually enriching relationships between Lutherans and Orthodox in Transylvania, attributed this positive relationality to the stability of the identities of the communities involved. Family-like relationships of nurturing reciprocity serve the basic human needs of Christian communities as they relate to other human communities. Recounting the story of Christians and Muslims in Jos, Nigeria, in 2001, Rebecca Samuel Dali reported on the two communities' tragic experience of hurting themselves in hurting each other. In contrast, Margaretha Hendriks described how the Indian Ocean tsunami made people realize that they need one another in times of tragedy and disaster. Even when identities are undergoing transformation in the service of greater justice, the instabilities of the process can lead to violence, as recounted by Sr. Miriam Noemi Francisco, OSB, of the Philippines. Observationally, these presentations lead to the prospect that working for peace in some settings calls for the church to enter into relationships of mutuality and interdependence with other communities, nurturing the stability of their identity. Here we come to a theological conundrum: how can we understand the church, the body of Christ, the foretaste of the final fulfilment of the Kingdom, as being called to relationships of mutuality and interdependence with, and also to affirm the identity of, communities of other religions, with secular society, not only with persons of good will but perhaps with persons of neutral will or even ill will?

Realizing mutuality and interdependence is possible only when human vulnerability is acknowledged as strength and possibility for the celebration of life in relationships. In Oslo, Sturla Stalsett emphasized the need to view this anthropological condition of vulnerability as an ethical precondition for responsible ways of human living: 'This is the essence of God's salvation in Jesus Christ, rooted in the assertion of powerlessness. God's power does not dominate or destroy, nor does it violate or victimize. It transforms persons and communities and the world through love and just relationships.'[16] Raag Rolfsen added: 'To be human is to be vulnerable and the human face is all the more beautiful when vulnerability marks its features.'[17]

However, vulnerability as an aspect of peace cannot be served out to all. This is a message that needs to be directed essentially to those who believe in and exercise power in autocratic ways. The wealthy and the powerful peoples and nations must learn again the gift of becoming vulnerable through God to each other and the created order as a whole. The theological knowledge of the '*kenosis* of Jesus' has concrete political implications. 'Jesus set himself as an example to his followers: to suffer with and not to ignore, to serve and not to dominate, to show compassion and not to justify violence.'[18] Thus, along with countering the prevailing myth that proclaims the invincibility and encourages the invulnerability of the powerful and rich, which is based on hubris and autonomy, it also calls into question the politics of immigration and trade, which are based on keeping the vulnerable out of strong economic nations.

The vulnerability of the weak and the poor, on the other hand, cannot be glorified as though it is the sanctified site that concretely signifies the kenotic God in an otherwise fallen world. Most often, their vulnerability has been purchased in blood without their consent by the pathologies of power that found regimes of structural violence. Peace requires that security be ensured to the poor and the marginalized as the first step towards negotiating in freedom what aspects of vulnerability they will pursue to keep them in a state of belonging to God and to each other as children of God in relatedness to all of creation. As Nobel laureate Amartya Sen puts it:

> We have to shift our attention from an exclusive concentration on incomes and commodities (often used in economic analyses) to things that people have reason to value intrinsically. Incomes and commodities are valued mainly as 'instruments' – as means to other ends. We desire them for what we can do with them; possessing commodities or income is not valuable in itself. Indeed, we seek income primarily for the help it might provide in leading a good life –a life we have reason to value.[19]

Survival of the poor and the oppressed can only be ensured by security for life against the effects of invincibility generated by the rich and powerful. But this does not mean that vulnerability is not needed for the poor and the dispossessed of the world. Their human capacity for vulnerability already gets exhibited in their trusting dependence on God, since all other powers are not trustworthy. Further, a sense of vulnerability to those who are weaker among them needs to be encouraged to keep them open to the longing for peace, which is marked by mutuality, interdependence and integral relatedness in God to each other and all of creation. There are multiple levels of vulnerabilities among the poor, too. Learning *kenosis* in the face of the human propensity to usurp power for self-gratification at the expense of the other also includes the poor at some level.

Peace mediates hope by liturgically linking lament with laughter

Peace comes from experiencing God's activity in the world (experience), which is witnessed to by God's word (scriptures) and which is testified to by God's faithful peace-seekers and peacemakers (tradition). The church is called not only to accept its vocation to be peacebearers and peacemakers in our violent world today, but is also commissioned ritually to create a sacred space for reconnecting with the key source of this connectedness (God) through which human beings can claim their relatedness to each other in a web of relationship that ties all of creation together.

The joy and hope, the grief and anxiety of all human persons are also the joy and hope, the grief and anxiety of the church.[20] According to the teachings of the Catholic bishops of the Second Vatican Council in their *Pastoral Constitution on the Church in the Modern*

World, Gaudium et Spes, all humanity shares a common origin and a common destiny in God. As was the first Adam, Christ the new Adam, in entering human history, united himself with all human beings.[21] The eucharist 'signifies what the world is to become: an offering and hymn of praise to the Creator, a universal communion in the body of Christ, a kingdom of justice, love and peace in the Holy Spirit'.[22] The eucharist is an *anamnesis*, a memorial of Christ. It remembers and makes available for us the Prince of Peace, the Holy One of God who through his own life and death overcomes violence: 'Christ himself with all that he has accomplished for us and for all creation (in his incarnation, servanthood, ministry, teaching, suffering, sacrifice, resurrection, ascension and sending of the Spirit)' is present in the memorial of him that we celebrate.[23] The entire action of the eucharist has an '*epikletic* character', invoking the Spirit's gift of peace (Galatians 5:22).[24] The celebration of the eucharist includes exchanges of a sign of peace, an indication of the centrality of peace as an element in the right ordering of relations among the human community participating in the celebration.[25] As the meal of the Kingdom,

> the eucharist opens up the vision of the divine rule which has been promised as the final renewal of creation, and is a foretaste of it. Signs of this renewal are present in the world wherever the grace of God is manifest and human beings work for justice, love and peace. The eucharist is the feast at which the church gives thanks to God for these signs and joyfully celebrates and anticipates the coming of the Kingdom in Christ (1 Corinthians 11:26; Matthew 26:29).[26]

In its ministry, the whole people of God 'are called to proclaim and prefigure the Kingdom of God. It accomplishes this by announcing the Gospel to the world and by its very existence as the body of Christ.'[27]

Worship, for all Christian communities across the world, is an occasion for reclaiming our primary rootedness in God through which we realize and release our mutuality and interdependence on other human beings and all of creation. This ritual space becomes a community site, which laments honestly at the disconnections that produce violence and laughs hopefully at the prospect of peace. In the eucharist, human brokenness elicits lament and God's gift of wholeness offered through Christ evokes the possibility of celebrative laughter. But this marriage of lament and laughter in the presence of God is central to the worship as a whole. The arrogance and pride of human beings and their desire for invulnerability, which lead to violation and violence, become the cause for lament and God's gracious gifts of love, grace and goodness, which lead to peace with justice, become the reason for celebratory laughter. This twin leitmotif runs through the entire Christian worship. The church needs creatively to reorganize its liturgical setting to aid the vocation of its members to be both peacebearers and peacemakers for Christ in the world. No longer can worship be distanced from the conflict, brokenness and fragmentation of the world. 'The biblical witness provides space for raw, naked honesty to be expressed in the presence of each other and God.'[28]

The rites of lament and laughter provide us with a twofold instrument to recall and celebrate our condition of belonging to each other as children of God in relatedness with all of creation within the arena of liturgy. Lament is a form of public weeping that combines complaint of the violated and broken ones, their trust in the faithfulness of God even in such conditions and their confidence in the possible repentance of the gathered community in a journey towards peace. 'For the hurt of my people I am hurt, I mourn, and dismay has taken hold of me. Is there no balm in Gilead? Is there no physician there? Why then has the health of my poor people not been restored?' (Jeremiah 8:21, 22). Lament is essential to the life of the poor and exploited both in biblical times and in the present. It is a catharsis that expels the pain, pathos, *han*, resentment, anger and despondency of the poor and the dispossessed. It is also a subtle form of truth telling that registers a complaint against members or sections of the community in the form of communicating neglect on the part of God. Wailing our protest to God is a veiled (and somewhat safe) form of blurting out truth at power. Lament is a collective ritual of forging solidarity among those who are dispossessed and taken advantage of in an unjust system. It calculatingly seeks partners in pain who want to challenge God and fellow human beings concerning their pain and brokenness. Interestingly, among the Dalits of South India, the drum symbolizes and generates lament. It is utilized by Dalits in public rituals to gather up the sufferings of the people and posit this into the heart of God/dess. The resounding beat of the drum collects protest, communicates this publicly before the whole community, and transports this to the Divine. Remarkably, *parai*, which means 'drum' in Tamil, is the root from which the English term pariah (outcaste) is derived. Pariah (the outcaste Dalit) then is to be understood as wailing drum-people. *Parai*, thus, is something of a wailing drum rather than a talking one – a disguised community symbol of the lament of the oppressed to God in front of the oppressive caste communities.[29] Lament is an act of hope that something can be done by God and God's children about oppression and marginalization. It must also be noted that lament is also a ritual that provides space for the powerful and the oppressor to weep before God and other human beings in contrition. It creates timely opportunities for the perpetrators of structural violence to listen to the cries of the poor for whom they are in some way responsible. It gives violent, violating protagonists the opportunity to repent and seek a new life of freedom from sin and guilt on the way to restoration for self and others. Lament, repentance and restoration give peace a chance for the whole community.

Laughter is the expression of joy in the presence of God. Before God, laughter seeks connection with the gift of joy that God can bestow upon the poor and the exploited. Before the public, laughter is used as a surviving device among the poor. It is a sense of humour that keeps the poor going when they are faced with intense economic hardship, political persecution and military repression. But laughter is also a means of unveiling the shallowness, immorality and illogic of brute violence on innocent peoples. It unmasks the foolishness and unethical nature of abusive power. It mocks at the destructive fascination for violence. Diego Irarrazaval from Chile, in a biblical reflection based on Luke 10:21, speaks of 'God's joy' and compares it to the sense of humour that the indigenous communities in South America, particularly in the highlands of Peru, exhibited in the face of intense hardship during political and military repression. 'They laughed at the shallowness of brute power that exercises itself on the powerless.'[30] It is this ritual of laughter that manifests the presence of God's gift of joy that mediates hope for the poor and the dispossessed. It does not communicate a deficiency that will be made good in an afterlife; rather, it mediates a foretaste that can keep hope alive so as to trust in and strive for peace with justice which also provides for forgiveness.

In the liturgy, which is the gathering together of all God's people, laughter can also be invitational to the rich and powerful members of the community. It offers to them the foretaste of a joy that can pervade their whole lives, if they too will commit themselves to peace. Laughter is not a joy in God that can be enjoyed separately from all God's people and God's creation. Rather, it is joy that exposes the enjoyment of those who laugh at the expense of others. It is the foretaste of peace as a condition of belonging and a state of longing: a condition of belonging to each other as children of God in relatedness with all of creation and a state of longing that joyfully joins in preparing for this eventual condition of relational blessedness. It becomes a gift of grace waiting to grow like a seed into a tree that brings forth peace-giving fruit. Laughter thus is a gift to the North and South, West and East, rich and poor, white and black, men and women, and privileged and deprived, which mediates hope in the potential of peace.

Peace is both a gift of God and a human work. Therefore, if peacebearing and peacemaking are forms of witness through which the church bears witness to the immanence and the fulfilment of the reign of God, then acts that promote mediation between justice and forgiveness, security and vulnerability, and lament and laughter in all situations of violence and human division become concrete possibilities.

As St. Cyprian of Carthage exhorts:[31]

Moreover, you have many things to ponder. Ponder paradise, where Cain, who destroyed his brother through jealousy, does not return. Ponder the kingdom of heaven to which the Lord admits only those of one heart and mind. Ponder the fact that only those can be called the sons of God who are peacemakers, who, united by divine birth and law, correspond to the likeness of God the Father and Christ. Ponder that we are under God's eyes, that we are running the course of our conversation, and life with God Himself looking on and judging, that then finally we can arrive at the point of succeeding in seeing Him, if we delight Him as He now observes us by our actions, if we show ourselves worthy of His grace and indulgence, if we, who are to please Him forever in heaven, please Him first in this world.

Issues for further reflection

1. Prospects for realizing mutuality and interdependence in situations marked by violent struggles for power, identities and resources.
2. *Koinonia* and *ecclesia* as models of mutuality and interdependence.
3. Overcoming violence as an opportunity for churches to be in partnership and solidarity across confessions and traditions.

Notes

Chapter 1

1. Rob Shropshire, in Hugh McCullum, *The Angels Have Left Us: The Rwanda Tragedy and the Churches*, Risk Book Series No. 66, World Council of Churches, Geneva, 1995.

2. 'Affirming Human Dignity, Rights of Peoples, and Integrity of Creation.' *Aide Memoire* of a theological consultation organized by the Faith and Order Commission of the World Council of Churches in Kigali, Rwanda, 4–9 December 2004.

3. As shared by a participant in Rwanda.

4. Robert McAfee Brown, *Religion and Violence*, Philadelphia, Westminster Press, 1987, p. 7.

5. 'Affirming Human Dignity, Rights of Peoples, and the Integrity of Creation', p. 2.

6. *Ibid.*, p. 10.

7. Mary Grey, 'The Integrity of Creation in the Context of the Spirit, Logic and Practice of Violence'. Paper presented at the Kigali consultation, pp. 2, 13.

8. 'Terrorism, Human Rights and Counter Terrorism.' Discussion paper for members of the CCIA Commission, presented at the 47th Meeting of the Commission of the Churches on International Affairs, World Council of Churches, Chavannes-de-Bogis, Switzerland, 14–19 June 2005, p. 3.

9. *Ibid.*

10. Grey, 'The Integrity of Creation', p. 2.

11. David J. Scheffer, US Ambassador-at-Large for War Crimes, 'Rape as a War Crime', Fordham University, New York, 29 October 1999. Posted on the website of Peace Movement Aotearoa at www.converge.org.nz/pma/arape.htm.

12. 'Some of us in this world kill our children, we abuse them sexually, we make them soldiers, we rape our women, we infect them with HIV/AIDS, we expose them to deadly diseases, and we make them work very hard and in hazardous conditions. We should all accept to be called Ammons and Herods.'

13. 'Mutuality and interdependence in a world of diverse identities: A Srilankan perspective.'

14. World Council of Churches, Commission of the Churches on International Affairs, *Human Rights: A Global Ecumenical Agenda*, World Council of Churches, Geneva, June 1993.

15. Kigali report, p. 3.

16. *Ibid.*, p. 9.

17. *Ibid.*, §83.

18. *Ibid.*, §94.

19. *Ibid.*, §83.

20. 'Reflections on the International Use of Power by the United States Government: A US Christian Contribution to the World Council of Churches' Decade to Overcome Violence', Washington, DC, 14 September 2005.

[21] Kigali report, §82.

[22] 'Ecumenical Perspectives on Theological Anthropology.' Faith and Order Standing Commission, Crete, 14–21 June 2005, §75.

[23] *Ibid.*, §80.

[24] *Ibid.*, §90.

[25] Ivone Gebara, *Longing for Running Water: Ecofeminism and Liberation*, Minneapolis, MN, Fortress Press, 1999, p. 83.

[26] Quoted in Grey, 'The Integrity of Creation', but originally found in Catherine Keller, *Apocalypse Now and Then: A Feminist Story of the End of the World*, Boston, MA, Beacon Press, 1996, p. 268, n. 108.

[27] This point was also made theologically in a groundbreaking study conducted by the Commission on International Affairs in the Church of Norway Council on Ecumenical and International Relations. The study was published as *Vulnerability and Security: Current Challenges in Security Policy from an Ethical and Theological Perspective.* The Norwegian text was published in 2000 and the English translation appeared in 2002.

[28] Statement of the Consultation on Theological Reflections on Overcoming Violence, Colombo, Sri Lanka, 12–18 November 1999, p. 6.

[29] See the statement 'The Protection of Endangered Populations in Situations of Armed Violence: Toward an Ecumenical Ethical Approach', WCC Central Committee, Potsdam, 29 January–6 February 2001.

[30] Konrad Raiser, 'The Responsibility to Protect'. Contribution to a public seminar in the context of an International Affairs and Advocacy Week organized by the WCC in New York, 13 November 2003.

[31] It is important not to exaggerate the convergence. There are still major tensions between the Christian pacifist tradition and the majority, just war tradition in Christian thought. See Fernando Enns, Scott Holland and Ann Riggs (eds), *Seeking Cultures of Peace: A Peace Church Conversation.* Telford, PA: Cascadia; Geneva: WCC; Scottdale: Herald Press, 2004, esp. Appendix 2: 'Just Peacemaking: Towards an Ecumenical Ethical Approach from the Perspective of the Historic Peace Churches.'

[32] *Herald Magazine*, 25 June, 2005, p. 18; Romeo Dallaire, *Shake Hands with the Devil*, London, Arrow, 2004.

[33] *Herald Magazine*, p. 20.

[34] 'Affirming Human Dignity, Rights of Peoples, and the Integrity of Creation', p. 13.

[35] See the 'Universal Declaration of Future Generation Rights of 1994', UNESCO and Equipe Cousteau, La Laguna, Tenerife, 26 February 1994, Art. 1, which states: 'Persons belonging to future generations have the right to an uncontaminated and undamaged Earth, including pure skies; they are entitled to its enjoyment as the ground of human history, of culture and of social bonds that make each generation and individual a member of one human family.'

[36] Edesio Sanchez, 'Power that Empowers – Power that Destroys.' Paper presented at a consultation on 'Interrogating and redefining power',

WCC and Faith and Order, Cret-Berard, Puidoux, Switzerland, 10–13 December 2003.

[37] 'Participation in God's Mission of Reconciliation, An Invitation to the Churches', Standing Commission on Faith and Order, Crete, Greece, June 2005, §87.

[38] 'Realizing mutuality and interdependence in a world of diverse identities.' *Aide Memoire* of a theological consultation organized by the Faith and Order Commission of the World Council of Churches in Oslo, Norway, 27–30 April 2005, p. 11.

[39] 'Nurturing peace, overcoming violence: In the way of Christ for the sake of the world.' Faith and Order Core Group on Theological Reflection on Peace, Cartigny, Switzerland, 2003, p. 4.

[40] As shared by a participant in Rwanda.

[41] 'Realizing Mutuality and Interdependence in a World of Diverse Identities', p. 11.

Chapter 2

[1] Nurturing Peace document.

[2] Konrad Raiser, "Rationale for a new ecumenical discourse on power', Cret-Berard report.

[3] See 'WCC General Secretary calls for a critical reassessment of the Cold-War period.' Press release, World Council of Churches, Geneva, 22 November 1999. See also 'WCC Acknowledges Inaction During Cold War; German Bishop Commemorates Coup'. *Christian Post*, San Francisco, 23 July 2004.

[4] Although the role of the WCC during that time has been studied, it warrants further reflection.

[5] See Duncan B. Forrester, *Truthful Action: Explanations in Practical Theology*, Edinburgh, T. & T. Clark, 2000, p. 81.

[6] 'Interrogating and Redefining Power.' Report of a theological consultation of younger theologians from the South organized by the Faith and Order Team of the World Council of Churches and the Faith, Mission and Unity Programme Area of the Christian Conference of Asia, Chiang Mai, Thailand, 23–28 February 2004.

[7] Nurturing Peace document.

[8] 'Participation in God's Mission of Reconciliation: An Invitation to the Churches.' Standing Commission on Faith and Order, Crete, Greece, June 2005, §74–8.

[9] Nurturing Peace document, p. 6.

[10] 'Reflections on the International Use of Power by the US Government: A US Christian Contribution to the WCC's DOV', Washington, DC, 14 September 2005 http://wcc-coe.org/wcc/what/faith/us-response-nurturingpeace.html).

[11] Ken Booth, 'Reasons of power and the power of reason: Some reflections from international politics', Cret-Berard consultation.

[12] For more on this, see the Chiang Mai report.

[13] For more on this, see chapter 2.

[14] See 'Interrogating and Redefining Power'. *Aide Memoire* of a theological consultation organized by the Faith and Order Team of the World Council of Churches in Cret-Berard, Puidoux, Switzerland, 10–13 December 2004.

[15] This raises another theological concern which should not be glossed over, and which requires further work: the effect of the images of a violent God in the biblical tradition, including the violent imagery of the apocalyptic writings. For a helpful engagement with this issue, see the essay by John Mansfield Prior SVD, 'The Conqueror and the Crucified: Reading the Book of Joshua in an Age of Terrorism'. In Michael A. Kelly CSSR and Mark A. O'Brien OP (eds), *Wisdom for Life*, Adelaide, Australia, ATF Press, 2005, pp. 57–75.

[16] Edesio Sanchez, 'Power that Empowers, Power that Destroys' (unpublished), p. 2.

[17] As narrated by Bishop Kumara Illangasinghe, 'Realizing mutuality and interdependence in a world of diverse identities'. *Aide Memoire* of a theological consultation organized by the Faith and Order Commission of the World Council of Churches in Oslo, Norway, 27–30 April 2005, p.6.

[18] Duncan B. Forrester, *Truthful Action: Explanations in Practical Theology*, Edinburgh, T. & T. Clark, 2000, p. 74.

[19] 'Participation in God's mission of reconciliation: An invitation to the churches.'

[20] Sanchez, 'Power that Empowers', pp. 1–5.

[21] 'Participation in God's mission of reconciliation', p. 12.

[22] Cret-Berard report, p. 10.

[23] Mary Grey, 'The Integrity of Creation in the Context of the Spirit, Logic and Practice of Violence'. Paper presented at the theological consultation in Kigali, Rwanda, December 2004, p. 11, with reference here to Carter Hayward, *Our Passion for Justice*, New York, Pilgrim Press, 1984.

[24] Forrester, *Truthful Action*, p. 77.

[25] Grey, 'The Integrity of Creation', p. 11.

[26] See Bell Hooks, who writes of wilderness space as 'a site of creativity and power, that inclusive space where we recover ourselves, where we move in solidarity to erase the category colonizer/colonized' and which 'offers one the possibility of radical perspective from which to see and create, to imagine alternatives, new worlds'. Bell Hooks, *Yearning: Race, Gender, and Cultural Politics*, Boston, MA, South End Press, 1990, pp. 152, 149–50.

[27] As Mark G. Brett, *Genesis: Procreation and the Politics of Identity*, Old Testament Readings, London, Routledge, 2000, p. 84, writes: 'Divine blessing flows extravagantly over the covenant's borders to include Ishmaelites …'

[28] See Carol A. Newsom, *The Book of Job: A Contest of Moral Imaginations*, Oxford, Oxford University Press, 2003.

84

[29] Cret-Berard document, p. 10.

[30] *Ibid.*

[31] Sanchez, 'Power that Empowers', p. 12.

[32] 'Interrogating and redefining power', Cret-Berard document, p. 10. See also the summary of Sturla Stalsett and Raag Rolfsen's paper on 'Vulnerability and security' in the *Aide Memoire*, 'Realizing mutuality and interdependence' from the theological consultation at Oslo, 27–30 April 2005, p. 2.

[33] *Ibid.*

[34] Grey, 'The Integrity of Creation', pp. 11–12. 'The Wild Bird who heals' is referenced to Mark Wallace's *Fragments of the Spirit*, New York, Continuum, 1996.

[35] Oslo report, p. 5.

[36] *Ibid.*

[37] *Ibid.*

[38] Especially 'Nurturing Peace, Overpowering Violence: In the way of Christ for the sake of the World' (2003); Konrad Raiser, 'Theological and Ethical Consideration on the Uses of Power in the Ecumenical Movement Today', CCIA 44th Meeting, Crans-Montana, Switzerland, 14–18 May 2001; 'Interrogating and Redefining Power', *Aide Memoire*, theological consultation organized in partnership with CCIA and JPIC (2003); 'Interrogating and Redefining Power', Consultation of Younger Theologians from the South, 2004; *Bulletin of the Program Area on Faith Mission and Unity (Theological Concerns): A Special Issue in Observance of the Decade to Overcome Violence*, Christian Conference of Asia, Vol. 20, No. 3, Chiang Mai, Thailand, December 2004.

[39] In biblical times, for instance, exilic prophets sought to empower people so that they might survive their persecution and displacement. Walter Brueggemann, *The Prophetic Imagination*, Philadelphia, Fortress Press, 1978, speaks of two moments of the prophetic imagination: the critical voice that identifies and the voice that provides alternatives and hopes. The latter is an example of the call to empower. Other figures have done the same in their various communities, such as Medha Patkar and Mahatama Gandhi in India; Martin Luther King Jr. and Malcom X among African-Americans in the USA; Wangari Mathai in Kenya; Te Whiti and Whina Cooper in Aotearoa-New Zealand; and many others at local levels.

[40] See the works of Paulo Freire on conscientizing, those of Emmanuel Levinas on facing the other, and Walter Wink's trilogy: *Naming the Powers, Unmasking the Powers, Engaging the Powers*, Minneapolis, MN, Fortress Press, 1984, 1986, 1992.

[41] See the works of Emmanual Levinas.

[42] See, for example, the works of Gustavo Gutiérrez.

[43] See Maya Angelou, *And Still I Rise*, New York, Random House, 1978.

[44] Mieke Bal has given her a name, *Bath*, a transliteration of the Hebrew word for daughter. For an alternative view on namelessness, see Jione

Havea, *Elusions of Control: Biblical Law on the Words of Women*, Leiden, Brill, 2003, pp. 99–127.

[45] See also Gemma Tulud Cruz, 'The Power of Resistance: A Look at the Power of the Powerless', *CTC Bulletin* 20 (3), 2004, pp. 131–7.

[46] There are several examples of what this call to empower to name entails. See, for example, the call to assert subjecthood in the 'Interrogating and Redefining Power' documents and Chan Ka Wai, 'Power is not Defined by What We Have', *CTC Bulletin* 20 (3), 2004, pp. 66–9. For affirmation of women in particular Southern contexts, see L. Jayachitra, 'Deconstructing Christ-Church Power Model: Enhancing the Dignity of Dalit Women in India', *CTC Bulletin* 20 (3), 2004, pp. 14–20; Eunice Karanja Kamaara, 'From Competition to Complementarity: Gender Reconstruction in Contemporary Africa', *CTC Bulletin* 20 (3), 2004, pp. 77–81; Joy Evelyn Abdul-Mohan, 'Caribbean Woman's Perspective of Empowerment', *CTC Bulletin* 20 (3), 2004, pp. 93–8.

[47] Chiang Mai report.

[48] See Aye New, 'Empowerment as Constructive Power for Gender Equality', *CTC Bulletin* 20 (3), 2004, pp. 82–7; Arnold Temple, 'Empowering for Fullness of Life', *CTC Bulletin* 20 (3), 2004, pp. 127–30; Forrester, *Truthful Action*, p. 81.

[49] See Raiser, 'Theological and Ethical Consideration', p. 2.

[50] 'Reflections on the International Use of Power by the US Government', p. 4.

[51] See Jione Havea, "Boring reading, forgotten readers", *Uniting Church Studies* 10 (2), 2004, pp. 22–36.

[52] See the 'Interrogating and Redefining Power' documents concerning the exercise of the power of interpretation, and Yani Yoo, 'How the Powerful Play their Bible Game (Numbers 12)', *CTC Bulletin* 20 (3), 2004, pp. 21–6.

[53] See the 'Interrogating and Redefining Power' documents concerning reimagining God and confronting the empire, as well as Alvin Gongora, 'Engaging the Powers: Meditations on Resistance from the Andean Region in South America', *CTC Bulletin* 20 (3), 2004, pp. 61–5; San No Thuan, 'Overcoming Oppression of Ethnic Minority Christians', *CTC Bulletin* 20 (3), 2004, pp. 113–19.

[54] Constitution of the United Nations Educational, Scientific and Cultural Organization, adopted in London on 16 November 1945, p. 7.

[55] Forrester, *Truthful Action*, pp. 73–89.

[56] See J. Harold Ellens VIII (ed.), *The Destructive Power of Religion: Violence in Judaism, Christianity and Islam*, Westport, CT, Praeger, 2004.

Chapter 3

[1] Nurturing Peace document, p. 7.

[2] Gennadios Limouris (ed.), *Church, Kingdom, World: The Church as Mystery and Prophetic Sign*. Faith and Order Paper No. 130, World Council of Churches, Geneva, 1986, p. 123.

86

3 Matthew 6:10; see *Church and World: The Unity of the Church and the Renewal of Human Community: A Faith and Order Study Document.* Faith and Order Paper No. 151, World Council of Churches, Geneva, 1990, II.29.

4 *Baptism, Eucharist and Ministry* (BEM), Faith and Order Paper No. 111, World Council of Churches, Geneva, 1982, B7.

5 BEM, B3. See also *Confessing the One Faith: An Ecumenical Explication of the Apostolic Faith as it is Confessed in the Nicene-Constantinopolitan Creed (381)*, Faith and Order Paper No. 153, World Council of Churches, Geneva, 1991, pp. 142–3, 146.

6 *The Nature and Mission of the Church – A Stage on the Way to a Common Statement* (TNMC), Revised Faith and Order Paper No. 181, Crete, 2005, §43.

7 See Thomas Merton, *Conjectures of a Guilty Bystander*, Garden City, NY, Doubleday, 1966.

8 TNMC, §52.

9 Cf. Faith and Order study on 'Ethnic Identity, National Identity and the Search for Unity'.

10 Jeffrey Gros and John D. Rempel (eds), *Fragmentation of the Church and its Unity in Peacemaking*, Grand Rapids, MI, Eerdmans, 2001, p. 222.

11 See Fernando Enns, Scott Holland and Ann K. Riggs (eds), *Seeking Cultures of Peace: A Peace Church Conversation*, Geneva, WCC, 2004, appendix 2, 'Just Peacemaking', p. 235.

12 'Nurturing Peace, Overcoming Violence', p. 9.

13 'Realizing Mutuality and Interdependence in a World of Diverse Identities.' *Aide Memoire* of a theological consultation organized by Faith and Order of the World Council of Churches in partnership with the Church of Norway and Norwegian Church Aid as a contribution to the Decade to Overcome Violence, Oslo, 27–30 April 2005, p. 11.

14 *Church and World*, Faith and Order Paper No. 151, Geneva, WCC, 1990, II §28.

15 'Realizing mutuality and interdependence in a world of diverse identities', p. 2.

16 *Ibid.*

17 'Realizing mutuality and interdependence in a world of diverse identities', p. 8.

18 Oslo report, p. 9.

19 Amartya Sen, "Mortality as an indicator of economic success and failure", *The Economic Journal*, 108 (January), London and Malden, Blackwell, 1998, p.2.

20 *GS* 1; Norman P. Tanner, *Decrees of the Ecumenical Councils*, London, Sheed & Ward; Washington, DC, Georgetown University Press, 1990, Vol. 2, p. 1069.

21 *GS* 22; Tanner, *Decrees of the Ecumenical Councils*, pp. 1081–3.

22 BEM, E4.

23 BEM, E6.

[24] BEM, E16, cf. E17–18.
[25] BEM, E21.
[26] BEM, E22.
[27] BEM, M4.
[28] 'Realizing mutuality and interdependence in a world of diverse identities', p. 10.
[29] It is important to keep in mind that while lament is a major theme in interpreting the *parai* drum, there is also another theme that is somewhat more subtle. This has to do with the rebellious dimension that the drum symbolizes. The *parai* drum was also used as an instrument to gather up courage in resistance. It energizes even for violent protest. Thus the *parai* drum is both a wailing and a waging symbol.
[30] 'Realizing mutuality and interdependence in a world of diverse identities', p. 3.
[31] St. Cyprian of Carthage, *Jealousy and Envy*, chapter 18, quoted in Hildo Bos & Jim Forest (eds.), *For the Peace from Above: An Orthodox Resource Book on War, Peace and Nationalism*, Syndesmos, Bialystok, 1999, p.59.